HIS
IN THE
SPIRIT

Confirmation Program

By
A Team of Daughters of St. Paul

St. Paul Books & Media

NIHIL OBSTAT:
Rev. Richard V. Lawlor, S.J.

IMPRIMATUR:
✠ Bernard Cardinal Law
Archbishop of Boston

AUTHORS:
The St. Paul Divine Master Religion Series was produced by a team of Daughters of St. Paul of the American Province in the spirit of the Servant of God, Reverend James Alberione, SSP, STD. The Sisters hold degrees in catechetics, theology, education, philosophy, communications and art.

THE TEAM OF AUTHORS:
Sr. Concetta Belleggia, M.A.
Sr. M. James Berger, B.A.
Sr. M. Anne Heffernan, M.A.
Sr. M. Helen Wallace, M.A
Sr. M. Mark Wickenhiser, M.A.

ART AND LAYOUT:
Sr. Annette M. Boccabello, A.A.S.
Sr. Virginia Helen Dick
Sr. Deborah Thomas Halpin
Sr. Clare Stephen Kralovic, B.A.
Sr. M. Alphonse Martineau
Sr. Rose William Pacatte, B.A.
Sr. M. Bernardine Sattler, B.A.

Scripture texts taken from the Revised Standard Version Bible (RSV) (modified form), Catholic Edition, copyrighted © 1965 and 1966 by the Division of Christian Education of the National Council of the Churches of Christ in the U.S.A., and used by permission.

PHOTO CREDITS:
A. Alvarez—57, 100, 128
American Indian Center, MO—195
Assumption Prep School—200
Canadian Pacific Railway—19
Cavanaugh—145
DSP—8, 12, 14, 18, 20, 22, 26, 28, 42, 52, 53, 54, 56, 61, 67, 69, 78, 79, 89, 90, 93, 99, 106, 107, 111, 112, 114, 120, 121, 122, 126, 130, 131 (top), 134, 136, 142, 144, 146, 149, 150, 151, 152, 156, 158, 160, 161, 169, 173, 176, 178, 180, 182, 184, 187, 190, 192, 193, 194, 197, 198, 202, 203, 204, 205, 206
DSP Philippines—29, 49, 129, 140, 175
Bruno del Priore—189
N. DiCarlo—133
Dore—33, 36, 37, 40, 58
Paul J. Elliott, Jr.—31

Jim Fashinell—6, 84, 147
Folla—45
HDC—162, 171, 172
Herman Nebel Studio—141
Hofman—27
Josephite Fathers 131 (bottom), 138
J. Kralovic—85
Lehmbeck—105
Phil Livingston—9
Mancusi—87
Arturo Mari—30, 74, 75, 76, 163, 169
R. Morrison—115
Murillo—25
St. Joseph's, Honey Creek—43
Msgr. Russell Terra—81, 82, 135, 196
Sr. Elizabeth Marie Tibbs, OSF—66
J. D. Tipfer—cover

ISBN 0-8198-3319-3   8 9   95 94 93 92

Printed in the U.S.A., by the Daughters of St. Paul
50 St. Paul's Ave., Boston, MA 02130

The Daughters of St. Paul are an international congregation of women religious serving the Church with the communications media.

Contents

What Confirmation Is All About

One Saturday morning a priest attended a meeting. The focus was on persons with physical and mental disabilities. This priest had been invited because the Church does so much for persons with disabilities.

The meeting was just beginning when Father arrived and took a seat in the back of the large conference room. The sessions continued uneventfully throughout the day. During the last session, however, the moderator wrote on the chalkboard, "Mental retardation is a moral evil."

The priest knew he could not let that statement go unchallenged. If enough people believed this, the day might come when the law could legally neglect helping disabled individuals. Persons with mental disabilities could be "outlawed" as moral evils. The results for such

persons and those who care for them would be devastating. Besides, the statement was absolutely false. Every human being is equally precious to God. The priest made this clear to the moderator.

"Father," came the answer, "there is no place for God in our meeting and discussions." The entire room was silent. Then, from a row of young people with various handicaps, a hand arose. The moderator had no choice but to call on the young man, who had an obvious mental disability. The young man looked at the moderator. He turned to the priest and back to the front again. He addressed the moderator: "I am different from you, and I don't know why. But I am made in the image and likeness of God, so there's nothing wrong with me."

What do you think of that young man's statement? Was it only that, a statement? No. This young man had obviously been taught the basics of Christian belief and had the courage to witness to it. What would you have done if you were in the same circumstances? Would you have had the courage to witness to your Faith as the priest and the young man did?

This is what Confirmation is all about. In Baptism original sin was washed from your soul and you received God's life. This life of God in the soul is called grace. In the sacrament of Penance or Reconciliation any sins committed after Baptism are forgiven, and grace is increased or restored to the soul. In the Holy Eucharist, Jesus Himself comes to live in us. When we are confirmed, we receive the Holy Spirit who comes to us in a special way to strengthen us in living the Christian life. In all the sacraments we receive God's life, His precious gift of grace.

In studying the Catholic Faith before receiving the sacrament of Confirmation you will be learning many new words and phrases. Don't get discouraged if you have to study a little harder than you had to in the past. It is worth the effort because what you are learning is for your own happiness in this life and in the next. Studying the Faith is a marvelous experience. When you know the Faith well, you will be able to find the key to making the right decisions in life, decisions that will determine your eternal happiness.

Throughout this book, you will find true life stories of people who daily faced the challenge of Christian living. Perhaps you will recognize yourself or people you know in these same or similar situations. The call to follow Christ as convinced Catholic Christians is for each of us, today and tomorrow. Therefore, we cannot help but admit the importance of knowing our Faith so we can live it.

You are young and perhaps impatient to get on with the business of living. But this special time in your life, preparing for the sacrament of Christian adulthood— Confirmation—is worth every moment you give to it. May God bless you!

The Search and the Goal

If we looked for one word that could best summarize what we all search for more than anything in the world, the word that best fits is: happiness. Some people are keenly aware of this relentless thirst. Others cannot express their desire in words, but the desire remains like the steady tick of a clock, or the constant rustle of a fall wind as it passes by our window.

No one can ignore that desire for happiness. The desire for happiness has been carved on our soul by the Creator Himself.

Why we are on this earth

The purpose of our life on earth is to be happy with the everlasting happiness that we can find only in God. Back in the fourth century, a restless, proud man finally admitted his need for the God who made him. He wrote: "Our hearts were made for You, O God, and ever restless will they be until they rest in You." Those words came from the hand of St. Augustine. His was a fascinating life.

Augustine, as a young man, had his share of problems. His family, though not wealthy, was comfortable according to the economic standards of northern Africa in the year 354. His father, Patricius, was an unbeliever. His mother, Monica, was a fervent Christian, an exemplary wife and mother. But to the young Augustine, his mother may have seemed to be overly religious.

Augustine and his companions were unruly and frequently found or caused trouble. From the time Augustine was seventeen, he led a life of moral and intellectual "freedom." Freedom in this case means *without control*. The last thing that this young man wanted was any kind of restraint. Yet, he was never happy, only empty.

Augustine wrote his life story in a book called the *Confessions*. This book is one of the most revealing testimonies of spiritual misery and eventual spiritual happiness ever written. It is also a real study of the human personality. In it, the future priest, bishop and saint tells of his boyhood, his teenage years, his sins and failures. But most of all, the *Confessions* is a brave account of one man's struggle to give up sinful pleasures to embrace Christianity.

When Augustine was twenty-nine, he went to Rome and opened a school. Yet, even though he was absorbed in his studies, he did not take his mind and heart off the real problem: his search for *happiness*. Looking back on those dark days and trivial pastimes, Augustine wrote: "That was my life, O my God, but was it *really* a life?"

God's grace, his mother's prayers and his own sincerity finally prevailed. One night, Augustine desperately prayed: "How long, O Lord, how long shall I go on saying *tomorrow* and again *tomorrow*? Why not have an end to my immoral living this very hour?" Earlier his mother had given him a copy of the *Letters of St. Paul.* He opened the book and read the passage from Romans in which St. Paul challenges the Christian to become holy (see: Romans 13:13-14).

Thus, at the age of thirty-two, Augustine was baptized. There followed a peaceful time of prayer with his mother. After her death, he returned to his native city of Tagaste and began to live a hidden, prayer-filled Christian life. Soon he was ordained a priest. He and other men desiring to follow Christ more closely chose to lead a common life. They renounced their possessions and began to follow the rule of life Augustine had established. Thus was born the Augustinian Order, still very much a part of the Church today.

But this was not all he did. As Bishop of Hippo, Augustine continually defended the Church against the *heresies* of his day and became one of the greatest philosophers and theologians of the Church. He wrote extensively. Augustine was a kind and holy bishop. And even if he had not done all this, and *become* all this, he would have left a great legacy. In one of his most famous sentences that captures the quest of every person who has ever lived or who will ever live, Augustine said: "How true it is, O Lord, that You have made us for Yourself, and our hearts are restless until they rest in You."

Fifteen centuries later, a college dropout, caught in the clutches of drug abuse and gambling, found peace for his tortured soul in prayer before the Blessed Sacrament. Jesus, in the tabernacle, gave him the strength to find peace of mind and stability. Looking back over his broken life, this British poet, Francis Thompson, wrote one of the most powerful poems in the English language. He pictured God, the loving Father, on a divine chase down London's back alleys and dirt-laden streets for the soul of one of His creatures. "The Hound of Heaven" is, in many ways, Thompson's autobiography.

St. Augustine and Francis Thompson lived hundreds of years apart, but they both had the same lesson to learn: only God can make us happy because He gave us such a great desire for happiness that nothing less than union with Him can satisfy us.

Finding happiness does not come automatically, however, like turning on the faucet and having running water. Because our eternal destiny is so great, God asks us to earn it with His help. So finding happiness and our eternal destiny are linked together. Total happiness, then, is rooted in God. But we can begin to share in God's happiness even now, by living in conformity to His will which brings peace of heart. But by far the greatest happiness will be enjoyed after death. It is then that the faithful person will hear:

"Well done, good and faithful servant. Enter into the joy of your master."

(Matthew 25:21)

How will I spend my life?

Being serious about finding true happiness in life involves three important steps: we must know, love and serve God every day of our lives.

I can know God by studying about Him. This calls for taking seriously my religion classes. It means doing the homework assigned. Above all, I must let what I believe influence the way I live my life. What I believe should make a difference in the way I think, speak and act. Living my Faith will make me a better person.

We can love and serve God mainly by:
—wanting to love and serve Him
—avoiding sin
—sharing in the sacramental life, especially the frequent reception of Penance and Eucharist
—remaining loyal to the teachings and laws of Christ's Church

—drawing others to Him by living a Christ-like life, and doing what we can to influence people toward embracing the Catholic Faith
—doing works of Christian service.

Where Jesus waits

Our souls will live forever either eternally happy with God in heaven or eternally damned. Jesus said: "Those who have done good, to the resurrection of life, and those who have done evil, to the resurrection of judgment" (John 5:29).

The thought of heaven should become a challenge to work for that goal and to help others reach it. Our salvation means so much to God. St. Paul wrote to the Romans:

"If God is for us, who is against us? He who did not spare his own Son but gave him up for us all, will he not also give us all things with him?"

(Romans 8:31-32)

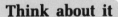

Think about it

You are preparing to receive the Holy Spirit in the sacrament of Confirmation. The Holy Spirit will make a big difference in your life if you prepare well to receive Him. Practice the three steps mentioned earlier in this chapter: know, love and serve God. Then when you receive the sacrament of Confirmation, the Holy Spirit will fortify you in your good desires. He will help you to become more fervent; He will inspire you to put God first in your life. Think of what He did for the first Apostles (see: Acts, chapter 2). Frightened, faltering men were changed into heroes who would eventually suffer even martyrdom for Jesus. Being a faithful Catholic has a "price." It costs us something, but think of the great reward...heaven.

Prayer

Come, Holy Spirit,
Touch my mind with the importance of the sacrament of Confirmation and my need for Your help.
Give my will the strength to choose what is best for my soul and not just what is easy or comfortable.
Fill my heart with love for the God who created, saves and sanctifies.
I give my life over to You and ask that You lead me along the course which in Your goodness, You have designed for me.
Stay with me; work with me. Amen.

I Believe...

- We can know God through reason and revelation; divine revelation is necessary.

- We can probe something of the mystery of God's life within Himself.

- God is the Creator of everything that exists: angels, human beings and all creation.

- Our first parents sinned; God promised a Redeemer.

- We reflect on the purpose of our life.

The "Reasonableness" of Belief

Every funeral home, every cemetery, attests to a fact we are inclined to think little about: some day each of us will die. Faced with this unbending reality, we automatically begin to consider the "prospects" of an afterlife. An "afterlife" would, of necessity, logically connect to a Supreme Being who is outside of death, who holds all life in His hands. The thinking individual who asks: is there a God? hears the reassuring answer: "Yes, there is a God." To the Ephesians, St. Paul wrote:

"There is...one God and Father of us all, who is above all and through all and in all" (4:6).

No definition can ever exhaust the marvel of God, and to define Him, we realize the need for human words. No human words, of course, are adequate, yet words are all we have and they can help us to form a concept about the good God who loves us and cares for us.

Who God is

God is the all-powerful Spirit who created everything that makes up the universe. He is real and living, and He is impossible to miss! How can that be, if He is invisible? St. Paul explains to the Romans:

"Ever since the creation of the world his invisible nature, namely, his eternal power and deity, has been clearly perceived in the things that have been made" (1:20).

The universe is the great "open book" of God in which we can witness His power and majesty. Our reason—the power by which we can think—points to the universe and says: "There has to be a Mastermind behind all this."

We can know about God's existence from nature's laws, the degrees of perfection in the universe, motion, causes and effects, and changing beings.

Our reason can tell us that God does exist and can give us some glimpses into His marvelous nature. For example, the universe's order and design suggest to us God's infinite intelligence. The intricate beauty in a new born baby's ear or eye is a lesson about the infinite perfection that can be found in God. Creation reflects God's infinite perfection.

At one time, Whittaker Chambers was an American Communist and an atheist. The story of his regained faith in God began when one day he sat watching his baby daughter eat breakfast. "My eye came to rest on those delicate ears, those intricate, perfect ears. The thought passed through my mind: '...they could have been created only by immense design.' The thought was involuntary and unwanted.... If I had completed it, I should have had to say: Design presupposes God."

There are also other religious facts we can know by the use of our reason: the human soul will never die; everyone has a duty to worship God, our Creator; the Gospels are real, historical books, worthy of being believed. We will be taking each of these important truths in later lessons.

But even if we push our human mind to the brink, or even if we implore the keenest and most intelligent human beings, we find the need for more help in knowing about God. That extra help has not been denied. It is called **revelation.**

Think about it

Some people walk through a part or all of their lives alone. A non-believer is a person who has not yet received, or has rejected, God's gift of faith. An atheist is a person who claims that there is no God or at least he lives as though there were no God. An agnostic is a person who thinks that he cannot know whether God exists or not. Belief in God or faith in God is a gift. Faith is like the pearl that Jesus spoke about in Matthew's Gospel. He said:

"The kingdom of heaven is like a merchant in search of fine pearls, who, on finding one pearl of great value, went and sold all that he had and bought it."

(Matthew 13:45-46)

God's revelation

Because our minds could only grasp "so much," God, in His goodness, told us about Himself, ourselves and His plan of love for us. Even though we can, with our human intelligence, reason to the existence of God, we cannot "reason" to the mystery of the Trinity or why God made us; why He created the universe; why He became a baby at Bethlehem and died on the cross; why He gave us His Mother to be our Mother; why He left us His Church. The divine "whys" could only be answered by revelation.

God's revelation is what He has told us about Himself, ourselves and His plan of love for us. Revelation is the sum of the truths of religion which God has made known to us through Sacred Scripture (the Bible) and Sacred Tradition (doctrinal content of our Faith passed on from generation to generation through the teaching authority of the Church).

A genuine need

Many times we can invent or imagine a physical need. But one need we all have, and it is a genuine spiritual need: the need to know the truth about God. We need God's revelation because without His help our reason (thinking power) could not discover everything that God wants us to know about Himself. We need revelation to know the truth about ourselves and His plan of salvation for us. The plan of salvation is for our present life and the life to come.

God has given us His revelation in various ways: first, through His Son, Jesus Christ, who is God-made-man. He has also revealed Himself through the Bible, divine Tradition and the teachings of the Church. The treasury of divine revelation is called the *Deposit of Faith*. The deposit of truths which God has revealed has been given to His Church to keep and to teach.

14

Think about it

The spiritual treasures God has revealed—called the Deposit of Faith—are like a banquet for our souls. This banquet is never diminished. We cannot say we are "finished" studying our Faith. There is always so much more to learn. Studying about our Catholic Faith helps us to nourish the gift of Faith by which we believe what God has revealed.

The Profession of Faith we recite every Sunday at Mass is our Creed. It is the Mass prayer in which we declare what we believe.

Evidence of Jesus in my life

I have been given many great gifts, especially my *mind* to think with and my *will* to make choices. How do I really use them? Do my thoughts and will choices bring me closer to Jesus?

Prayer

God my Father, You have given
me a mind that can reason and a
will that can freely choose to accept or reject You.
Give me the grace to always
choose You, to use my mind to
know You, my will to keep close
to You, my sentiments to love
You, who are my Creator and Redeemer.
Remind me to say often with St. Augustine:
"You have made me for Yourself,
O Lord, and my heart is restless
until it rests in You."

Mystery and Marvel— What God Is Like

How to describe God

When we want to find out information about a particular topic, we go to the sources. We research our topic in encyclopedias and in books specializing in that field of information. What if our research topic is God Himself? Where do we go for information? We recall from the previous chapter that our source is divine Revelation: what God has told us about Himself in Sacred Scripture and Sacred Tradition.

God is perfect. By perfect we mean that God is almighty, eternal, all-present, all-good, all-knowing, all-merciful and all-just. God can do all things. Perfect means without any kind of blemish or weakness. Yet, that still is not enough to describe God. A word that somewhat captures God's unlimited perfection is **infinite.** How can we describe infinite? Infinite means perfect, without

limitation. Jesus said: "'For God all things are possible'" (Matthew 19:26). In God there is not even a "shadow" of change (see: James 1:17). So we say infinite describes perfect and perfect describes infinite. We are caught in a "maze" of words. We realize, then, that we are merely human beings, so small in comparison to God.

The God who cares

When we ponder God's nature, we learn how to be humble. We see ourselves as we are: God's creatures. He loves each of us. He calls us each by name.

Why do we feel so small and insignificant when we think about God and our relationship to Him? Because we owe our existence and all that we have and are to Him. Without His love and care for us, we would not even exist.

Mystery of the One in Three

Who hasn't encountered "mystery" before? A mystery is something we cannot fully grasp. In religion, a mystery is a great truth revealed by God which our limited minds will never be able to wholly understand. God has told us about the mystery of the Blessed Trinity. He has revealed Himself to be three Persons in one God—our Triune God, the Trinity. Looking at Sacred Scripture, we see hints of the doctrine of the Trinity in the Old Testament. In Genesis 1:26, God said: "Let us make man."

Jesus Himself clearly introduced us to the doctrine of the Trinity in the New Testament. Just before His ascension, the Lord said to the eleven:

"All authority in heaven and on earth has been given to me. Go therefore and make disciples of all nations, baptizing them in the name of the Father and of the Son and of the Holy Spirit" (Matthew 28:18-19).

The mystery of the Blessed Trinity is that there is one God in three divine Persons—Father, Son and the Holy Spirit. The Father is God and the first Person of the Blessed Trinity. The Son is God and the second Person of the Blessed Trinity. The Holy Spirit is God and the third Person of the Blessed Trinity. We can never totally understand the mystery of the Blessed Trinity. No human being can totally understand the Trinity because that would require an infinite mind. But to think about the wonder of this mystery teaches us so much.

We can understand *something* of the mystery of the Trinity. By one God we mean the one divine nature, while by "three Persons" we mean the Father, Son and Holy Spirit, who possess the divine nature. This wonderful mystery was well-known in the early Church, among the first Christians. It is spoken of clearly in the Apostles' Creed, which has been in existence since the time of the Apostles.

17

The Trinity in my life

Every mystery has meaning for us. A supernatural mystery is important. When we think of the Trinity in relation to the afterlife, we each can say: the three Persons of the Trinity call me to everlasting happiness with them. Imagine how wonderful heaven will be with God the Father, God the Son, and God the Holy Spirit. Then we can find the answer to the mysteries of life, death and eternity. In heaven all our desires will be fulfilled and our desire for happiness fully satisfied.

At Baptism, the Blessed Trinity came to live within us. If we grow in grace through prayer, the reception of the sacraments and virtuous living, we will draw closer to our Triune God throughout life, and will earn eternal union with God in heaven.

In heaven, we will be able to ask God Himself how He can be one and three.

Evidence of Jesus in my life

If I should find that I am too concerned with my own importance, I will ask Jesus for the grace to become humble enough to admit that God is the Center of the universe, not me.

Prayer

God, the Holy Trinity, because
You are goodness, You have room
for me in Your loving embrace.
Because You are mercy, You
forgive my sins and offenses.
Because You are all-knowing, You
understand me through and through.
Because You are all-just and fair,
I ask that You keep me far from sin.
Teach me how to love You.
My God, help me.

God's Cherished Creatures

God our Father, the first Person of the Blessed Trinity, is also called the Creator. There is so much we can know about God's creation, yet, there remains so much to learn. Perhaps some of the answers to these secrets will be ours when we are finally at home forever with God.

Because God is God, and is, therefore, infinite, He can do all things. He can create. To create means to bring something out of nothing—which only God can do. The next time you are out in your backyard, or even better are walking down a street, look at the sky, the trees, the animals and, above all, at the people you pass by. Think that these creatures reflect the goodness of God their Creator. How different the world around us becomes if we see God at the center of everything.

God created all the matter and energy in the universe, as well as the pure spirits called angels and each of us. God created the world out of His immense, infinite goodness, and to share His perfections with us.

But what if we walk down some streets of a city or town in any part of the world and see burned-out houses, smashed windows, garbage and litter along the sides of the streets? How can we call the world beautiful? The world still is beautiful because all that God made is good. Sometimes, however, His gifts are misused or wasted by the free choice of human beings. We can avoid such ingratitude in our own lives when we form the habit of thinking of God as our Creator and Father, and by thanking Him for all His gifts, and acting accordingly.

The angels

It is so easy to set our sights only on the material things in our lives, in other words: on what we can see, hear, taste, smell and touch. Yet, beyond our senses is a whole spiritual world, truly a real world of existence where God's creatures without bodies dwell. Who are these creatures and what are they called? They are called angels. The angels play a large role in salvation history, in God's saving actions in the lives of human beings. We find angels in the Old Testament and New Testament books of the Bible.

Angels are spirits, or real spiritual beings, without bodies. They have understanding and free will, just as we do. When it comes to spiritual realities, we can know very little from our human reason or thinking power alone. We need the facts that God tells us, that God has revealed to us. This message to us, contained in the Bible and sacred Church teaching, is called divine Revelation. We cannot prove from reason alone that angels exist, yet, the existence of angels is not contrary to reason. Why? It is very "reasonable" to suggest that just as there are creatures composed totally of matter (rocks, plants and animals), and creatures made up of matter and spirit (human beings), so it is right that there should be purely spiritual creatures.

Angels are often referred to in common language. Have you ever heard or used such expressions as: "She looks like an angel," or "She acts like an angel"? The word angel is equated with a person who is good. Even these popular expressions justly fit the faithful angels. Angels are not human beings, but they are persons. Persons are beings with intelligence and free will. The angels were created intelligent and free. The faithful angels who chose to be true to God certainly are good angels. This calls for some explanation.

When God created the angels— the exact number of which is not known—He gave them special gifts of supernatural grace, wisdom, power and holiness. They were also given the opportunity to merit heaven, that is, the direct vision of God, by remaining faithful to Him.

The test

In the Bible we see that not all of the angels remained faithful. St. Peter, the first Pope, writes: "...God did not spare the angels when they sinned, but cast them into hell..." (2 Peter 2:4). The angels were put to some kind of a test. The unfaithful angels who rebelled against God were sent to hell. They are called devils or evil spirits (see: Matthew 25:41).

The faithful angels were admitted to the face-to-face presence of God, which means they behold God directly. This is also called the *Beatific Vision*. These good angels see, love and adore God eternally, and live in close union with Him.

After their test, there remained the victorious and the vanquished angels. And all this has a repercussion on us. We know about some of the good angels who helped people in Biblical times especially by praying for them, and by bringing messages from God to them (see: Exodus 23:20, Tobit 5, Luke 1:28), and by being their guardian angels. Some angels are archangels. From the Bible we know the names of three: Michael, Raphael and Gabriel.

The unfaithful angels who rebelled against God were sent to hell. These devils or evil spirits try to harm us chiefly by tempting us to sin. Other temptations come from ourselves—our wounded human nature, a result of *original sin*, and from the persons and things around us. We can resist any and all temptations, though, if we pray and ask God's help (see: 1 Corinthians 10:12-13).

Think about it

It has often been said that nothing worthwhile is accomplished without a struggle. Imagine, then, the struggle and prayer required to live close to God on this earth—to remain in His grace—so as to be with Him for all eternity. The next time the goal seems too remote, or the road too steep, remember your guardian angel, your own protector. Ask him to smooth the road and to reinforce your will power.

Evidence of Jesus in my life

Perhaps I have not formed this good habit yet, but to help myself daily to keep my commitment to God in view, I can say the prayer: *Angel of God* frequently. (See page 211.)

Prayer

Father in heaven, my Creator,
You have given me so many
   wonderful gifts.
The sad fact is that I take so
   much for granted.
One of Your most treasured
   gifts to me is my guardian
   angel.
It is true that I rarely think of
   his sacred presence and so I
   fail to ask his help.
But that is all changed now.
From this day onward,
I thank You for my angel's
   constant protection.

Human Failure
and a God Who Loves

Our triune God was and is totally happy. He does not need creatures to add to His happiness. Yet, He created angels, human beings and the whole universe. Why? Since God is infinite Intelligence, He must have a motive for acting. Why did God create rational creatures: angels and human beings? Not because He was lonely, not because He needed us, not just to populate the earth, but out of love. It was total unselfish love, the infinite love of God that gave us life. Every angel can say: God's love caused my existence. Every human being can say: God's love caused my existence.

The first man and woman, Adam and Eve, were the created fruits of God's infinite love. What an ideal situation they lived in. Yet, sad to say, sin entered the human story and drastically changed humanity's relationship with its Creator. Our first parents were human beings composed of body and soul. Adam and Eve were the first parents of the entire human race. Chapters one through four of Genesis, the Bible's first book, manifest God's great love for human beings:

"God created man in his own
    image;
in the image of God he created
    him" (Genesis 1:27).

God lavished gifts on our first parents such as: natural happiness, knowledge, passions controlled by reason, and freedom from suffering and death. But the most important gift given to our first parents by God was sanctifying grace.

Adam and Eve were truly blessed to have these gifts freely given. But even in that bliss, they did not and could not behold the Beatific Vision. God gave our first parents natural life and many gifts. They, like the angels, had intelligence and free will. God would permit them to be tested to prove their fidelity to Him. Adam and Eve were capable of sinning because they had been given a free will. To sin means to purposely disobey God's law and will.

Chapter three of Genesis gives the account of our first parents' unfaithfulness. "So the woman saw that the tree was good for food, and that it was a delight for the eyes, and that the tree was to be desired to make one wise, she took of its fruit and ate; and she also gave some to her husband, and he ate" (Genesis 3:6).

Think about it

Temptation is part of everyone's life. Temptations (suggestions to sin), no matter how powerful, are not sins in themselves. We can learn a great lesson from Eve's conversation with the devil who was disguised as a serpent. Eve lost ground from the very start. She stopped to converse with the devil. She listened to his tempting proposition. "You will not die. For God knows that when you eat of it your eyes will be opened, and you will be like God, knowing good and evil" (Genesis 3:4-5).

Eve let the devil's suggestion play in her mind. She knew it was against God's command, but still.... Perhaps she could devise some kind of compromise. Then, she made her decision.

Eve ate the forbidden fruit, took it to Adam and he ate the fruit, too. Adam and Eve had committed the first sin in the human story (see: Genesis 3:6).

Consequences

We, no doubt, have all found out at one time or another, that sin has its consequences. Guilt, remorse, anxiety, sorrow wind their way around our lives. Sin is a serious matter. Adam and Eve soon faced the reality of separation from God...the saddest state for any human being. The cunning serpent that glittered in the sun never even hinted about the consequences of our first parents' sin. Because of that act of disobedience— which marked their ingratitude to an infinite loving God—our first parents lost sanctifying grace, the right to heaven, and the gifts they had received. They became subject to suffering and death, felt strong inclinations to evil, and were driven from the garden of paradise.

The sin of Adam and Eve in us is called original sin. Original sin can best be defined as the lack of grace with which each of us comes into the world, because our first parents lost grace both for themselves and for us.

Mary, Jesus' Mother, in view of the merits of her divine Son, was preserved from original sin from the moment of her conception in the womb of her mother. This great privilege is called the Immaculate Conception. It was proclaimed a dogma of faith by Pope Pius IX in 1854, and the feast commemorating this truth is celebrated every year on December 8.

The story of the fall of our first parents does involve us, then. But how can we be part of that first sad event if we did not yet even exist? Adam's descendants, in the plan of God, would have received the special gifts God gave to Adam and to Eve. So when our first parents lost those gifts, they were lost for us, too.

Sometimes we find ourselves easily attracted to evil, to laziness, to greed, selfishness and vice. Why? Certainly, God did not create us in this weakened condition. Our nature has been wounded—not depraved—but wounded by original sin. When we know about original sin and recognize its effects, we seek the spiritual helps of prayer and the sacraments to overcome them. Any human weakness of ours can be overcome in Christ. St. Paul explained that point a long time ago to the Romans:

"For if many died through one man's trespass, much more have the grace of God and the free gift in the grace of that one man Jesus Christ abounded for many."

(Romans 5:15)

God begins His work in us at Baptism. God our Creator, Savior and Sanctifier gives His grace to us and is actively present in our lives in our thoughts, decisions and actions. The most perfect way that we can cooperate with God in this life is to become holy, that is, to do His will as perfectly as we can and bring other people to Him.

Think about it

Each of us is a very real part of the loving story of God's creation. Each of us is a very real part of salvation history. God has entrusted us with existence, time, intelligence, will power, physical and moral gifts, and our Catholic Faith. If until now, we might not have appreciated God's saving work in our lives, let us begin today to tell Him often of our gratitude and ask Him to teach us to never forget the lesson of our first parents.

Evidence of Jesus in my life

To orientate each day toward God and to resist inevitable temptations to sin, I renew my determination to say morning and evening prayers every day.

Prayer

Lord, all around me people
    seem to be rushing in a
    thousand directions, caught
    up in the things that count
    for making this life easier
    and more successful.
Help me to strengthen my
    grasp of what is expected of
    me as a Catholic, and never
    to give time to the "serpent."
    When I am tempted, remind
    me to pray.
When I am lonely, hurt,
    annoyed, and turned in on
    my own small world, please
    reach down, straighten me
    up and direct my course.
Increase my faith in Your Son,
    Jesus, and lead me to Him.

The Mystery of Jesus

The authentic sources of Scripture and Tradition reveal:

- Who Jesus Is
- Jesus' divine and human origins
- How Jesus is our Savior
- Jesus' miracles and prophecies
- the Resurrection—Jesus' greatest miracle
- Jesus as the Divine Teacher

Who Are You Really?

Much emphasis is given to *roots* and *origins*. Individuals want to be part of a heritage and history. Racial and ethnic groups preserve distinct characteristics and customs of their cultures. *Roots* and *origins* in our spiritual life take us as Catholics to the heart of our belief. At the core and center of our Faith is a person—*Jesus*. People construct many images of Jesus; they say many different things about *who* He was; *what* He taught; *how* He lived and what His *living* and *dying* mean for each of us personally. We can learn so much about Jesus. The important thing is to seek our information from the right sources.

It is reasonable to believe that before He went back to heaven, Jesus would have entrusted the preservation of His true image to a reliable authority that would outlive and outlast the normal life span of any one human being. What better reason for Jesus to establish His Church that could and would offer people the means to gain eternal life until the end of time.

Could this happen? *Would* this happen? To both these questions we answer: "yes." Jesus remains present even today, nearly 2,000 years later, in His Church.

Sacred Scripture or the Bible is God's own Word, written down by men who were guided by the Holy Spirit. It is our Father's letter to us.

Sacred Tradition is the teachings of Jesus, or of the Apostles illumined by the Holy Spirit, that were not written by the first Christians but passed on from the apostles through their successors. Tradition was later written down, mainly in the official teachings of the Church.

Divine or Sacred Tradition has also been described as the process by which the Church, through the assistance of the Holy Spirit, in her teaching, life and worship, keeps continually ever-present, and hands on to all generations, all that she is and all that she believes.

In the sacred deposit, *Sacred Scripture* and *Sacred Tradition*, we find the treasure of our Catholic belief. Looking at Sacred Scripture, we see that there are four books of the Bible which tell us about the life of Jesus. These books are the Gospels of Matthew, Mark, Luke and John. The more we read and reverence these sacred books, the more we will know and live the Jesus of the Gospels. When we read these books with reverence we are challenged to become disciples of Jesus, the Teacher. If we open our hearts to Him, really and totally trust Him, Jesus will gradually become the center of our life.

This presupposes:
— good will on our part to seek and find Jesus
— prayerful effort to root out from our lives what cannot exist in the lives of authentic followers of Christ
— the desire to want to study about and become closer to Jesus all of our life
— the desire to share our Faith with others.

Think about it

Today's secularistic attitudes, reinforced by constant media bombardment, do not permit us the "luxury" of being uncommitted Christians. If we are uncommitted Christians, we will be swept downstream with the current. How do we row against the current? By praying to always increase our faith and by making the right choices that will keep us close to Jesus the Teacher.

Finding Him...

Sun-baked roads, soft breezes, the bright glare of the afternoon sun...and people everywhere. They were young and old, healthy and sick, serene or troubled, good living or sinners, all joined together by a single mutual interest—Jesus of Nazareth. He had many followers, and from that group of disciples, He selected twelve men who would be schooled in a particularly close manner. We call these men *Apostles*.

We can imagine ourselves to be part of that crowd who listened to the Master. Would we have remained just spectators, or would we have become part of the more interested group of disciples? What would we

have seen in Jesus of Nazareth? What would we have hoped for? What would we have thought He would do for us?

The crowds who *watched* and *listened* nearly 2,000 years ago witnessed in action the greatest Teacher who ever lived. We can even be tempted to be a little envious of those who listened to Jesus and walked with Him. Yet, do we really have to be envious? Not at all, because we who have been given the gift of faith, and are nourished by the *sacraments*, which are the saving actions of Jesus, have the opportunity of making Him the most important Person in our lives.

Who is Jesus?

Who is Jesus? What do we know about Him? He is God the Son, the second Person of the Blessed Trinity, who became man to save us from sin.

Jesus was always God, but He was not always a man. The name we give to His taking of a human body and soul is the *Incarnation*. Jesus became "incarnate" in Mary's womb (see: Matthew 2:1; Luke 1:31, 35; 2:72), and was born in Bethlehem.

Jesus will remain both God and man forever. He is only one Person, and that Person is God the Son. Because He has two natures—God's nature and a human nature—He is both God and man. We can help ourselves to appreciate the significance of this great truth about Christ if we look at two words of the definition: *nature* and *person*. A *nature* is *what* something or someone is; a *person* is *who* someone is. Jesus is one Person with two natures. Jesus is still both God and man and will continue to be so forever.

Think about it

In regard to Jesus, *nature* answers *what* He is: *divine* and *human*. Person answers *who* He is. He is Jesus Christ. In regard to you: nature answers *what* you are—a human being; person answers *who* you are, a particular individual with a name, a distinct personality and characteristics.

God and man

Jesus, then, is God and man. This is a great mystery of our Faith. Jesus, the Messiah or Savior, became a man to be our Redeemer.

Those crowds watching Jesus on the hillsides did not know what we, as Catholics, could one day know about Him. We receive what has been given to us through the treasury of the Church's Sacred Scripture and Tradition. *Jesus is truly God and truly man.* This is a unique combination that has occurred only once, and will never be duplicated. *Hypostatic Union* is a term used to describe the union of Jesus' divine nature and His human nature in one Person, the second Person of the Blessed Trinity.

Think about it

Jesus is the Light of the World. "The real light which gives light to every man was coming into the world" (John 1:9). We can think of the *light* as *grace*, or God's life in us, and *darkness* as *sin*. The only way we can lose God's grace is by sinning. But Jesus gives us the strength to walk in His light and to let His light shine through to others whom we meet. When we pray and keep in contact with Jesus, we become mirrors of His light.

Evidence of Jesus in my life

Do I sometimes catch myself thirsting for attention and desiring to be the "light"? At such moments, I will remind myself that Jesus is the true "Light," and He must shine through me.

Prayer

Jesus Master, once You spoke unforgettable words to Your disciples about being the light of the world. You called Yourself the Light and said that we, too, must be the light. You told us to be lamps of faith burning bright, reflections of the goodness of Your Father in heaven (see: Matthew 5:14-16).

Make me a *reflector* of Your light so that those around me, beginning with my family, my relatives and friends, may find at least a little bit of You in me.

Come and See

Mary, the Mother of Jesus, and St. Elizabeth were cousins. John the Baptizer was the son of Elizabeth and Zachary. We read about the extraordinary circumstances surrounding John's birth in chapter one of Luke's Gospel. John was a great prophet, but he was not the Messiah. He led his disciples and those who would listen to him to Jesus (see: John 1:29).

Among the first to follow Jesus were Andrew and his brother Simon Peter. These two men, who would be numbered among the original twelve apostles, were sincere, hardworking fishermen.

Andrew found Jesus first. In his enthusiasm, he went to get his brother Simon, and led him to the Master. Andrew exclaimed: "We found the Messiah!" (see: John 1:41) Simon Peter, the man who would become the visible head of Jesus' Church, went with Andrew to see this Rabbi, this Teacher whom people were already calling the Messiah. The Messiah was the great leader foretold in the Old Testament who would set up God's kingdom on earth.

A savior is one who saves, that is, who frees people from sins and brings them to God. The name Jesus means God saves, or the Savior (see: Matthew 1:21). Christ means the Messiah.

Jesus' human origins

Jesus' Mother was the Blessed Virgin Mary, a Jewish girl from Nazareth. An ancient tradition tells us that her parents were Sts. Joachim and Anne. Jesus did not have a human father. Jesus' Father is God. St. Joseph was Jesus' foster father and His guardian.

At every Eucharistic Celebration in which we pray the Creed, or when we recite the Apostles' Creed, we express our belief in Jesus who was conceived by the Holy Spirit, and born of the Virgin Mary.

The Son of God became a man at the moment in which Mary agreed to become His Mother. The second Person of the Blessed Trinity took on a human body and soul in Mary's womb, through the power of the Holy Spirit.

The conception of Jesus in Mary's womb is celebrated with the feast of the Annunciation. By Annunciation is meant the day on which the Church recalls the Angel Gabriel's announcement to Mary, her acceptance, and the Incarnation of the Son.

Think about it

John the Baptizer and the Blessed Mother of God are great people of faith who show us how to seek and find Jesus. We can learn, too, from the trust and enthusiasm of Andrew and Simon Peter. God working in our lives can do marvels for us. As Mary, as John the Baptizer, as Andrew, as Simon Peter, we put our trust in Jesus, God's Son, and then we, too, can exclaim:

"Behold the Lamb of God
who takes away the sins of the
world!"

(John 1:29)

The Savior's secret message

We celebrate the birthday of this special Person every year on December 25. Some people only think of gifts, decorated trees, feasts and fun. Still others think of it solely as a family time. Christmas is or can be all of these and yet the secret of the day lies deeper, beneath the surface, away from the noise and the fun. We find the true meaning of Christmas when we stop to gaze at a manger scene. And what do we see? A stable; a few animals; a manger with straw. Above all, we see people: Mary and Joseph and the Baby lying in the straw. We might also see shepherds and the three wise men who followed the star.

Stop...really stop the next time you see a manger scene and think about, reflect on what you see. Then read about the event in Matthew 1:18-25; 2:1-12 and Luke 2:1-20. As we read and meditate, we realize that Jesus, the Son of God, was born in an animal shelter. He was born of the Virgin Mary. Mary is really the Mother of God, because she is the Mother of Jesus who is God. Our Lady remained a virgin before, during and after the birth of Christ. This privilege is called the Virgin-birth.

Evidence of Jesus in my life

If I find myself seeking possessions and "things" in a desperate search for happiness, then I should often think about the poverty of Jesus, who is God, born in a stable. This will help me to gradually change my mentality and seek after spiritual things that last forever. .

Prayer

Jesus, You were once a baby in Bethlehem.

I can honestly admit that I think too little about the time You spent on this earth.

You chose to be poor and shunned sophistication and attitudes of superiority.

And You are God.

You know me—how proud and possessive I am.

You know how much the values of the world have penetrated my choices and my life style.

I am a follower, not a leader.

Transform me, divine Teacher, into a true and lasting follower of Yours.

Divine Dilemma

Jesus, the Master, was, is and will remain for all time a Teacher. He taught the people of His time; He teaches us what to believe and the right way to live. Above all, He came to earth to redeem us. We human beings had offended our Creator through our first parents (see: Genesis, chapters 1—4). Adam and Eve had sinned. To sin means to purposely disobey God's law and will. There are two kinds of sin: *original* and *personal*. The sin our first parents passed on to us is called *original sin. Personal sins* may be *mortal* or *venial*; they are sins which we ourselves commit.

Original sin, as explained in an earlier lesson, may best be described as the lack of grace with which each of us comes into the world because our first parents lost grace both for themselves and for us. Our first parents, as representatives of the human race, lost sanctifying grace, the right to heaven and the gifts they had received. They became subject to suffering and death, felt strong inclinations to evil, and were driven from the garden of paradise.

The problem God solved

The seriousness of an offense is measured in proportion to the person who is offended. Our first parents had offended God. Adam and Eve were human beings, not divine. How could they ever make up or repair for the offense? Alone, they would not be able to. God can infinitely repair for an offense to Himself. Yet, human beings had committed the offense; justice required that they pay the price. How would the dilemma be solved? Only God could have devised such a solution. He sent His only Son to save us (see: 1 John 4:9-10).

36

God solved the problem of how we could be redeemed or bought back by sending His Son—divine and human—to save us.

Salvation history started at the time of our first parents, who sinned seriously and lost God's grace for themselves and their descendants. Sin began to spread in the world, but God did not leave the human race. Again and again, He offered a covenant to His people. Through the prophets He kept alive the promise of the Redeemer's coming to save us. When the right time came, He sent His Son to die for our sins and gave us the chance of obtaining the happiness of heaven.

Even in our time, until the end of time, by the working of the Holy Spirit, God continues to bring all people the salvation that Jesus won for us on Calvary's cross.

The Savior of all people is Jesus Christ.

Think about it

Some people, sometimes even ourselves, try to get away with doing the least. We might settle for following the road that requires the least effort. That is when we should look for the example of someone who did the most, not the least. That Person who always did the most, even to the point of dying on the cross for us, is Jesus.

The Jesus who walked this earth

He was full of mystery, yet so easy to feel close to, so easy to trust. He inspired confidence in people. He looked for the good in everyone. He found motives for loving each person who crossed His path. He taught with authority. He taught as no Rabbi ever had.

He was straightforward, honest, precise. Yet, in His compassionate understanding of the uniqueness of each person, He sought out the "gold" in each one. With divine tact, Jesus gently challenged a person to become the best part of himself or herself. His followers grew; His disciples multiplied. People from all walks of life and backgrounds found Him, followed Him, sought His advice. One such person was Nicodemus.

Chapter three of St. John's Gospel records the conversation of Jesus and Nicodemus. In the course of that conversation, Jesus said that whoever believes in God's Son will never die, but will have eternal life (see: John 3:16).

Nicodemus was afraid of what others might think and say, but he needed the Master's help. He trusted the advice and wanted to enjoy the conversation of the Master. He valued the Lord's company. But he did not want to admit it to himself or to others. That is why he came to Jesus "at night."

What a lesson Jesus can teach us here. He saw Nicodemus clear through. He knew everything that the Pharisee was thinking, but Jesus accepted Nicodemus the way he was. Jesus sat with him, counseled him, and showed that He was convinced of Nicodemus' worth.

Think about it

Jesus is God. Just as He knew Nicodemus totally, so He knows each one of us. He loves us individually; He died for us individually, personally. He waits in the tabernacle, in the Blessed Sacrament of the Eucharist, for us to come to Him, to seek His advice, to ask for strength to remain true to our commitments.

Evidence of Jesus in my life

Jesus spoke words of wisdom and goodness to Nicodemus who came to converse with Him. I, too, can converse with Jesus often, every day, whenever I pray. Do I frequently take advantage of the gift of prayer?

Prayer

Jesus, Teacher, just as You spent time in conversation, instructing Nicodemus, I, too, want to learn the value of divine conversation with You. Speak to my soul. Make me ready to listen as Nicodemus was. Help me to admit that what You say to me is what I really need so that I may become what You want me to be. And even if what You say calls for a change in my life, I want to do it with all my heart. Make me a good listener as Nicodemus was; most of all, teach me to do Your will.

What He Did and Why

If you had lived nearly two thousand years ago in the little town of Nazareth, you would have seen Jesus, a hard-working boy, going to the well for water, doing many other necessary chores and helping His foster-father in the carpenter shop. He would have been doing whatever was required of the child of a laborer. The people in Nazareth did not know that Jesus was anyone other than an ordinary human being. He did not outwardly manifest or portray His divinity in any way. St. Luke sums up those first thirty years easily by stating that Jesus advanced in wisdom, age and grace (see: Luke 2:52).

Jesus' public life is His life of teaching. That public life ended with Jesus' death and resurrection. Jesus taught many things during His public life. He taught by the words that He spoke and the actions He performed.

If we study the Gospels carefully, we will see that Jesus is truly God. In ways that were very clear for the people of His time and country, Jesus showed that He was God. He backed up His claim to be God by *working miracles* and by *prophesying*.

A *miracle* is something that takes place outside of the ordinary working of nature's laws—something only God can do, because He made the laws. God can do anything that is possible,

compassion, at the invitation of His Mother, turn ordinary water into delicious wine. The wedding at Cana is the first of Jesus' miracles (see: John 2:2-11).

"If you believe..."

Cana in Galilee must have been special to the Divine Master because it was to witness the faith of a pagan royal official. Galilee was also to witness the cure of the man's son who was at the point of death. Even though still at his home in Capernaum, the boy was cured. We can picture the royal official. No doubt he was dressed well, a gentleman. He was trained to hide his emotions in the face of duty. But besides being a royal official, he was foremost a father. His son was critically ill, beyond the help of doctors. The boy would die unless God would intervene.

The royal official heard about the Wonder Worker, about Jesus. Once more, a glimmer of hope shone in his anxious eyes. Somehow he knew that if he could just meet the Teacher, Jesus would cure his son. And so the royal official went to Cana, worked his way through the crowd that listened to the Master, and made his request. "Come to see my son before he dies," the man said. Jesus' words were soft and sure: "Go back to your home," He replied. "Your son is going to live." The royal official looked into the Master's eyes. He believed that his son would live. Peace filled his soul as he started down the road that led home (see: John 4:49-50). The royal official's faith had moved the heart of Jesus. The royal official's trust led the Divine Master to work a miracle.

anything, in other words, that is not contradictory in itself. For example, God cannot and will not create a square circle, because the nature of a circle is to be round, not square.

A *prophecy* is such because it foretells or interprets correctly a future event that is subject to the free will of God or human beings. Jesus prophesied His own resurrection (see: Mark 10:32-34). In the next chapter, other prophecies of Jesus will be pointed out.

The Gospels record many of the miracles that Jesus performed. We see the Divine Teacher, filled with

Think about it

All through Jesus' public life, there is one quality that moves His heart above all others. It is the thread that weaves its way throughout the Gospels, the golden thread of *faith*. Still today that gift is given to those who seek it. A woman whose name we do not know passed one day through Lourdes, France. She was on her way to a fashionable seaside resort on the Riviera. She was a Catholic, but when her husband had died a few years before, she had lost all her belief in God.

Lourdes had been the scene of the appearances of the Blessed Virgin Mary to the teenager, Bernadette Soubirous, in 1858. A great shrine had been built there to honor the Mother of God and many cures have taken place. Even today, Lourdes remains the most visited Christian shrine in the world.

This particular woman was very impressed by what she saw at Lourdes: the faith of the people, the happiness on the faces of the elderly and the suffering. Her curiosity led her to stay in Lourdes for a few days.... Today if you go to Lourdes, you will see a statue of a blind man who had just recovered his sight. Indeed, the first miracle that took place at Lourdes was exactly that— the cure of a blind man. But this statue, a true monument, stands for more than that. A lonely, heart-broken woman had the statue erected in gratitude for what the Lord had done for her. She regained her *faith* at the Lourdes shrine. That is why the inscription at the base of the statue reads:

To recover faith is a greater miracle than to recover sight!

The miracles of Jesus

The Gospels are filled with the wonders that Jesus of Nazareth performed. He walked on the sea (see: John 6:19). He multiplied bread and fish to feed the hungry crowds (see: John 6:1-15; 6:25-59); He cured people caught in physical infirmities.

One of the most delightful episodes in all the Gospels is given a whole chapter—chapter nine—by John: "The Man Born Blind." Jesus cast out devils (see: Mark 1:22-28) and even restored dead people to life (see: John, chapter 11).

While we remain in awe at the wonders Jesus performed, we can reflect, too, on the concluding sentence of St. John's Gospel:

"There are still many other things that Jesus did, yet if they were written about in detail, I doubt there would be room enough in the entire world to hold the books to record them."

(21:25)

Jesus, the Divine Master, being human as well as divine, understood each person whom He met. He read right into the troubled eyes of each one and saw the hidden sufferings, the torments, the fears, imaginary or real, the physical pain, the sin and guilt and good will. He saw each person for what he or she really was and He loved each one with a personal love.

Evidence of Jesus in my life

Many times I want to become more spiritual; I want to grow in faith and trust. It is not easy. At those moments, I will remember that Jesus said to *ask, seek* and *knock* (see: Luke 11:9), and will ask His infinite help.

Prayer

Jesus, Divine Teacher, You have so much to give me if I will just come to You and ask. You have what I need to be really happy in this life as well as in the next life. If I just ask, You will increase my faith. If I am sorry, You will forgive my sins. If I am lonely and weak and full of selfishness, You will help me to rise above my humanness. You will help me to become what I should. Lord, I trust You. Help me.

The Greatest Miracle

Jesus rose from the dead

Every miracle is great precisely because it is a miracle. The miracles Jesus performed are so important because they testify to the *truth* of His words and the *truth* of His life (see: John 5:36-37).

Jesus' words and actions testified to His divinity. But the most overwhelming proof—the greatest of His miracles—was His own resurrection. When the Apostle Thomas saw the risen Jesus, he adored Him as God. Jesus let him do this, which again shows that He was divine (see: John 20:24-29).

What is the miracle of Jesus' resurrection? Jesus came back to life again after His death on the cross. Jesus, truly human as well as divine, died on Calvary. His side was pierced by the soldier's lance (see: John 19:34). He was prepared for burial and His sacred body was laid in a borrowed tomb (see: John 19:38-42).

But the story of Jesus of Nazareth does not end there in the shadow of the cross, in the borrowed tomb, in the silence of death. There was a cross. There was a borrowed tomb. There was silence. But there was no defeat.

There would be victory! There would be Easter morning.

Importance of Jesus' resurrection

The resurrection of Jesus, which can be considered a fulfillment of a prophecy as well, is the Father's ultimate seal of credibility on God the Son. Jesus also prophesied His passion as well as the resurrection (see: Mark 10:32-34), His denial by Peter (see: John 13:36-38), and the destruction of the temple of Jerusalem, the pride and glory of the Hebrew nation (see: Mark 13:1-2), which took place about forty years after His ascension.

The *miracles* and *prophecies* of Jesus could only have been performed if God was with Him and had thus confirmed what He said about Himself being divine.

The Winged Man—
St. Matthew

The Lion—
St. Mark

The Ox—
St. Luke

The Eagle—
St. John

Think about it

The Gospels reveal to us the marvelous Person of Jesus of Nazareth. These four books of the New Testament: Matthew, Mark, Luke and John, clearly show that Jesus is truly God. The Gospels also show that Jesus was truly a man. From the Gospels we can see that Jesus grew from infancy to manhood, and He was sometimes hungry, thirsty and tired. In the Garden of Gethsemane, He prayed that His Father's will, not His own, be done—which showed that He had a human will distinct from His divine will. What can we learn from all this? That Jesus, the God-man, is the model for us to imitate. We learn how to imitate Jesus by meditating the Gospels. Those who imitate Jesus learn to be very self-sacrificing and brave.

The chaplain dies not

During the winter of 1942, World War II raged. Seven hundred and fifty Americans were on a Japanese ship heading for Japan. They were prisoners of war. Since their capture, Father Joseph Lafleur was a mainstay in the prisoners' darkest moments. Already awarded the *Distinguished Service Cross* for heroism in previous battles—dragging the wounded to safety, helping doctors give medical care to those who needed it—Father Lafleur did not stop now. When his time ran out, he re-enlisted. And now he was a prisoner of war with the men who needed him. The men remember that as long as Father Lafleur had bread and wine he said Mass. As long as he had clothes on his back, he gave a more needy man something to wear. His watch and eyeglasses were traded off for medicine.

Joseph Lafleur had always wanted to be a priest. At fourteen, he entered the minor seminary at St. Benedict, Louisiana. He was popular, athletic, always happy and a good student. Lafleur especially enjoyed French military history. With dramatic eloquence, Joseph would recite the last words of Marshal Michel Ney: "Come, see how a soldier dies in battle, but he dies not."

Father was ordained in 1938. Three years later when war broke out he realized the soldiers would need a priest. So he volunteered and was sent to Clark Field, Philippines.

Bombardments, battles and finally capture followed. First the prisoners had to clear jungle land. Then the fateful orders came. Seven hundred fifty prisoners were to be sent to Japan for work. Chaplain

Lafleur traded places with one of the men chosen for the job. After all, the prisoners would need a priest. So seven hundred fifty men—hungry, overworked, and nearly naked—were crammed into the hold of a Japanese ship which set sail for the Land of the Rising Sun. Three weeks later, the ship was torpedoed by an American submarine. The Americans would have been trapped, with no hope of escape, but a kind Japanese officer hurried to open the door of the hold.

"Father, hurry!" The excited Americans urged their chaplain to climb the ladder to freedom. He refused. Helping the other men up, Chaplain Lafleur remained near the door. He could not know how few of the men would survive the short swim to shore. Some Japanese sailors began throwing grenades into the ship's hold, and many Americans were shot on deck as they tried to reach the water. Only eighty Americans made it safely to land, and they are the ones who drew that final picture of their young chaplain, standing near the ladder helping others.

45

Evidence of Jesus in my life

The Divine Teacher told the Apostle Thomas not to persist in unbelief (see: John 20:27). Those words are meant for me, too. My faith in Jesus should be so much stronger than it is. Frequently, I will say in my heart: "My Lord, You are my God!"

Prayer

Jesus, Divine Teacher, You cannot be sectioned off or divided up. When people are truly Your followers, their whole being is affected: their mind, their will choices, the sentiments of their heart, their actions. Help me, Lord, to become a total Christian. I have a long way to go, but You will make the journey with me to Calvary and beyond Calvary, to the resurrection—my own personal resurrection in You.

The Goodness and Power of Jesus

After Jesus was baptized by John in the Jordan, the Holy Spirit hovered over Jesus, in the form of a dove, and the Father said: "This is my beloved Son in whom I am well pleased" (Matthew 3:17).

As the Divine Teacher walked the streets and hills of Palestine during the years of His public ministry, the Gospel events permit us glimpses into the goodness and power of the God-man. He was an eloquent speaker who taught with authority and could hold the crowds spellbound (see: Mark 1:22). He preached a life of purity, self-denial, obedience to the Ten Commandments.

He said He came, not to abolish the Old Testament law, but to fulfill it.

Chapters five to seven of Matthew's Gospel are called the *Sermon on the Mount*. In that sermon, Jesus spoke out against ambition, greed, hypocrisy. He spoke about being pure in our thoughts as well as our actions; about right intention in performing religious actions; about the evil of uncontrolled anger; about passing judgment on others.

Jesus said: "If you want to avoid judgment, stop passing judgment. Your verdict on others will be the verdict passed on you" (Matthew 7:1-2).

47

He preached the power of prayer. "Ask, and it will be given you; seek, and you will find; knock, and it will be opened to you" (Matthew 7:7). Jesus proposed to those who were eagerly listening to His Word, not a life of ease, of fun, of luxury, but a life of true peace and real joy to be found in ways they would never have imagined. This He would sum up in the eight Beatitudes (see: Matthew 5:3-11).

Jesus knew that down through the centuries, the Church would have many *saints*, many *martyrs*, too, who would prove the Beatitudes true. And there are martyrs for Christ in our own day who suffer for their belief in the Divine Teacher, who are persecuted by regimes and secular ideologies that are totally incompatible with Christianity and Catholicism. Still, they stand fast in their Faith, just as the Master before them, and they are "blessed."

Jesus could have preached a popular Christianity, a popular Catholicism. Many more people would probably have listened. Many more would probably have followed Him. He could have proclaimed Himself an earthly king. He could have defeated—without weapons—the mighty Roman Empire. Yet, He did not. He chose a humble life, a hard life, a poor life, a self-sacrificing life to teach us many important lessons.

Jesus went up and down Galilee preaching the "Good News," or *Gospel*. Why was it good news if He preached self-denial, forgiveness of enemies, fidelity in marriage until death, a lifetime of searching for "heavenly treasure"? It was Jesus who said: "You cannot give yourself to God and money" (Matthew 6:24). These concepts and much more formed the message of the Divine Teacher. It was indeed good news because those who would *listen* and *believe*, would be able to change their lives for the better and elevate their whole being, becoming people with *spiritual goals* and *values*.

Think about it

Jesus, God's Son, could have had a luxurious life. He rightly should have been acclaimed by the contemporary kings and caesars. As the Creator, He should have been offered the very best that this world could give. But Jesus, the King of kings, chose a different kind of life. He wanted to serve others, not to be served.

Divine secrets

The Divine Teacher offered people the secrets of His Father's kingdom. He told *parables* (delightful stories with a good moral) about self-sacrificing love, the Father's mercy, and about eternal life. He was a "master" storyteller. His characters are so real that those who listened then and those who still listen to the Gospel parables today are fascinated.

Who can remain unmoved by the lavish father of the famous "Prodigal Son"? (see: Luke 15:1-31). Who is not edified by the compassion of the man known to history as the Good Samaritan? (see: Luke 10:25-37). Jesus' stories go to the very hearts of His listeners because the characters He talked about are real. The father of the Prodigal Son is God and the son is any one of us who has sinned.

Jesus shows us that just as the Prodigal Son was totally forgiven by his father, so our heavenly Father forgives us our sins when we are sorry and are resolved to amend our lives. Well-known sinners like the Samaritan woman (see: John, chapter 4), and the penitent woman (see: Luke 7:36-56), found compassion and hope. To the penitent woman, Jesus spoke of forgiveness and salvation (see: Luke 7:50).

Jesus, who called Himself the Good Shepherd, showed tender mercy toward any and all who humbly acknowledged their sins and asked His help. The woman caught in adultery was brought by the Pharisees to Jesus (see: John 8:1-11). Seeing sorrow in her heart, He simply told her to be on her way and to stop sinning (see: John 8:11).

49

Evidence of Jesus in my life

My faith in Jesus is His gift to me (see: Matthew 10:8). I want to think of this fact and thank the Divine Teacher for faith by living my religion with sincere dedication and joy.

Prayer

Jesus, Divine Teacher, I want to pray often the prayer that You taught Your Apostles:

The Lord's Prayer
Our Father, who art in heaven, hallowed by Thy name; Thy kingdom come; Thy will be done on earth as it is in heaven. Give us this day our daily bread; and forgive us our trespasses as we forgive those who trespass against us; and lead us not into temptation but deliver us from evil. Amen.

Our Savior Paid the Price

Why Jesus suffered...

- the Agony in the Garden
- the Scourging at the Pillar
- the Crowning with Thorns
- the Carrying of the Cross
- the Crucifixion

The Agony in the Garden

The night was chilly and dark. The Twelve Apostles had spent the day with Jesus. They had joined Him in the Last Supper and had watched Him change bread and wine into His own Body and Blood. He had said many penetrating things (see: John chapters 14-17) which seemed almost like a legacy. "But what did all of this mean?" the Apostles must have asked themselves. What did the *events* and *words* of the first Holy Thursday signify?

Now the small group, with Jesus in the lead, made their way to the Garden of Olives where Jesus liked to pray. "Watch and pray," the Master said to the Apostles, "so that you will not enter into temptation" (see: Matthew 26:41; Mark 14:38; Luke 22:40).

The Apostles were eleven because Judas had gone his own way. As they settled on the hard, damp earth, each one's eyes were rivoted on the Teacher. What a long day it had been. The Eleven were tired. During the day they had walked, listened, prayed together and feasted. By human standards, it was time to rest. But the Master was wrapped in prayer, in conversation with His heavenly Father. And He expected them to do the same.

Think about it

Prayer is talking with God. We can see how important prayer is when we study the Gospels which record the life of Jesus. No one ever worked harder than the Master. No one ever accomplished more in a day than He. Yet, He always made "holy" the best of times—the joyful times and the sad times—with prayer. Jesus' example challenges each of us. We ask ourselves: how willing am I to make prayer the most important part of my daily life? Why not begin today to give prayer the importance it deserves?

Jesus tastes the cup of suffering

As the Lord talked to His heavenly Father, He could foresee all the sufferings He would be enduring through that long Holy Thursday night and Good Friday. Because of His true human nature, Jesus was afraid. His prayer became a petition: "Father," He begged, "if you are willing, remove this cup from me; nevertheless not my will, but yours be done" (Luke 22:42). The cup which the Master refers to is the "cup of suffering."

But there was another reason, too, for Jesus' agony in the garden. All during that torturous ordeal, He could see the past, back to the beginning of the world, the present and the future, to the very last moment of the world's existence. Because Jesus is God, He also saw every sin that had been committed, every sin that would be committed, sins forgiven and unforgiven, sins of weakness, sins of malice, the sins of every human being who ever lived or would live. He felt the terrible weight of those sins placed on Him. The pressure of such intense sorrow caused the Divine Master to sweat drops of blood from every pore. His

Father sent angels to console Jesus (see: Luke 22:44), and Peter and the Apostles should have consoled Him, too. They didn't, though, because they were asleep.

Three times Jesus woke them and told them to pray (see: Mark 14:32-42). But the cold, hard ground looked more inviting than spending the night in prayer. So the Apostles slept on.

Judas and a band of soldiers were suddenly there. They wanted to arrest Jesus. What had He done? Why was it happening? How could He let it happen? The Apostles were awake now. They had slept when they needed the spiritual strength that comes from prayer. Now they would play the coward's role and run away, abandoning their Master, and preferring the obscurity of the night.

53

Think about it

What more could the Master possibly suffer? He saw in that agony in the Garden of Olives all that He would suffer. He saw, too, that after His suffering and death, some would reject His gift of redemption. Who would be such a fool as to toss aside the Master's gift of grace? We know that following Christ has a price. And so we ask Him that by His agony in the garden and His sweating of blood that we may learn to be sensitive to His great personal love for each of us. And, above all, we resolve to pray when we are tempted to betray Jesus by sinning.

Fear led the Apostles to run away and leave Jesus to His enemies. All but Judas repented and confessed their sorrow to Him. We learn from this never to despair of sins we have already committed, but to seek Jesus' forgiveness in the sacrament of Penance or Reconciliation.

Evidence of Jesus in my life

I will try to push away distractions at prayer and will make myself more aware of God's presence, especially when I am assisting at the Eucharistic Celebration.

Prayer

Many times, even most of the time, I judge events on the surface. I forget about the most real world of all—the world of the spiritual life of grace. You "purchased" that real world for me by Your death on the cross. Never let me betray You by sinning. But if I do, give me the courage to seek Your pardon in the sacrament of Penance. Remind me to pray and never to sleep when I should be praying. Amen.

Why Jesus suffered...

The Scourging at the Pillar

Holy Thursday night turned slowly into Good Friday morning. Jesus was dragged from the court of the High Priest to the palace of the Roman governor, Pontius Pilate. He was no doubt seeing Jesus for the first time. What a difference that meeting would make on Pilate's whole life. Two facts about him we do know for sure: first, he did not believe that Jesus is God. Secondly, even though he doubted Jesus' divinity, one thing he did not doubt: Jesus' innocence. The Master had done nothing deserving of death. But the crowds, stirred up by instigators, were clamoring for Jesus' death.

Pilate feared the crowd especially because some began to shout: "If you release this man, you are not Caesar's friend!" (John 19:12). In an effort to please them, Pilate turned Jesus over to the scourgers. Roman flogging, he knew, was so brutal that the blood-thirsty crowd would have their satisfaction. And yet, Jesus' life would still be spared. This was Pilate's first decision which would lead him down the bitter road of compromise.

It is said that of all the physical sufferings the Master endured, the scourging at the pillar was the most painful. And every part of Jesus' passion atoned or made up for particular kinds of sins committed freely by mankind.

During Jesus' bloody scourging while tied to a pillar and flogged with the Roman flagellum*, the Savior was atoning in a special way for sins of impurity: impure thoughts, impure words, impure actions. And because sins of impurity are often the result of weakness rather than malice, Jesus, by His scourging at the pillar, obtained for us the grace to be strong when we are tempted.

---

*A leather whip with sharp bits of iron lodged in the thongs at the end of the cords.

55

Jesus reminds us to pray for His grace to overcome any and all temptations. He asks us to think about what He suffered in His scourging at the pillar when bits of His flesh were ripped from His body, causing Him incredible pain. Jesus suffered this so that we would be sorry for any sins of impurity already committed and confess them in the sacrament of Penance. Then pray for the grace every day never to offend Jesus again.

Pilate's sad lesson

Everything the Divine Master said and did while He lived on this earth was said and done for a reason. His passion and His death on the cross provide us with a wonderful "book" of spiritual lessons.

Pilate was willing to compromise justice by permitting an innocent man to be scourged. Pilate also took advantage of a Roman custom to forgive and release a prisoner at the approach of a religious feast. His plan was to compare Jesus to the most notorious criminal he could find and offer the two prisoners to the crowd hoping that they would, of course, prefer Jesus. So the crowd was given the power to choose freedom for one only: Jesus or the notorious Barabbas.

Jesus was innocent. He was God's Son become man. He was the Master who had multiplied bread to feed a great multitude. He had given sight to the blind and hearing to the deaf. This was the Jesus who had healed infirmities of every sort, spiritual as well as physical. This was the Jesus of whom the crowds had been *spellbound* by His teachings (see: Matthew 22:33).

Barabbas, instead, was a revolutionary and a known murderer. His very name struck fear in any who heard it. Yet to him the crowd gave their blessing: "A long life to you, Barabbas!" and to Jesus the cross. Irrational world!

Think about it

When we really begin to reflect on what the Divine Teacher went through during His passion and death, it can change our own life forever. If each one of us would take even five minutes a day to read about or think over something Jesus suffered, it would help us never to compromise our love for Jesus.

Evidence of Jesus in my life

If I ever have to suffer unjustly, I can remember the example of Jesus. He permitted grave injustice to be committed against Him, and yet, He blessed and prayed for His persecutors.

Prayer

Divine Teacher, never again let me lose control over myself. Don't let me speak and act in ways that offend You. I don't want to join that frenzied crowd who called for Your death. But I do just that each time I sin. When I am weak, when I am tempted, give the grace to overcome all temptations by prayer. Give me the strength to make little acts of self-denial to help You shoulder Your cross to Calvary.

The Crowning with Thorns

The soldiers who flogged Jesus did not know restraint. Yet, if we think about it, they could hardly have been moved by hatred for the Person of Christ. They barely knew whom He was. They had probably only heard rumors of His incredible public ministry. Those soldiers, no doubt loosened by strong wine and bad habits, vented their wrath on a victim who could not (or would not) defend Himself.

Human justice won no victory that day or Jesus would never have been flogged in the first place. And now an added act of cruelty was done to Jesus.

Playing on the idea that Jesus had been considered by some as the King of the Jews, the soldiers took a thorn branch, wove it into a *crown* and pressed it onto His sacred head. The soldiers then placed a reed,

scepter-like, into His tied hands and threw the purple cloak, a mock symbol of royalty, around Him.

The soldiers bowed low, shouting: "Hail, King of the Jews!" They even spat on Him. Through it all, the Master said not a word. The soldiers tired finally and returned the "King" to Pilate who looked with compassion at Jesus' pitiful condition.

There He was, lacerated, bruised and bleeding, with the purple rag on His shoulders and the crown of thorns on His head. Hoping that the rage of the people would cool when they, too, had seen Him, Pilate presented Jesus to them saying: "Here is the man" (see: John 19:5). But even then the crowd would not back down. "Crucify Him!" they called. "Crucify Him!"

Pilate procrastinated when he should have made a firm and quick decision in Jesus' regard. How can an innocent man be scourged and beaten beyond recognition? How can an innocent man have thorns pushed into his skull? How can he be led to crucifixion? Yet, all this did happen, and the innocent Man it happened to was our God. Why did Jesus allow this to happen to Himself? What was His motivation? His motivation was *love*—love for each one of us. His motivation was *atonement for our sins.*

Pilate's final action

Pilate interrogated Jesus one last time. The Lord stood in silence. The procurator became impatient and reminded Jesus of his power to have the prisoner crucified. But Jesus quickly reminded Pilate that any power of his had been given from above (see: John 19:10-11).

How mysterious this poor, persecuted Man was. Reduced to such misery, who could be afraid of Him? Yet, somehow Pilate was afraid. But Pilate was afraid of the crowd, too. He was afraid of being reported to Rome. He feared for his position and his reputation. So he condemned the innocent Christ to death.

Evidence of Jesus in my life

I will reflect on the crowning with thorns and face the reality that life is a struggle. Jesus warned against *false prophets* (see: Matthew 7:15). I want to form strong convictions so that the "false prophets" of sex and drugs for pleasure and all the rest will not find me easy prey.

Prayer

Lord, I don't know what destiny was Pilate's. You have forgiven him, too, if he sought that forgiveness. But I do know about me. So many times, even without the presence of an angry mob, for human respect or because of spiritual laziness, I have betrayed You. I want to remember always the example of Pontius Pilate and pray every day never to compromise again.

The Carrying of the Cross

Our redemption is a serious thing. What have been some of the torments that Jesus suffered thus far? The mental anguish of feeling abandoned by His heavenly Father, the betrayal of Judas, the abandonment by the other Apostles. Peter's threefold denial made the Lord suffer very much and caused Peter bitter remorse (see: Luke 22:54-62). But Peter's denial has an important message for each of us: no sin is ever too serious or too grave or too big to be forgiven. No one need ever be without hope. We never want to despair as Judas did. Instead, we want to always go toward Christ as Peter. Peter remained until the end of his life keenly aware of his mistakes. Let us, too, seek the Lord's forgiveness.

The Divine Teacher will never turn away from us, if we are truly sorry. He will never stop loving us.

All four evangelists record that Pilate condemned Jesus to death (see: Matthew 27; Mark 15; Luke 23; John 19). Because He did not enjoy the privilege of being a Roman citizen, the Master could be crucified. And because He would permit the maximum punishment to be done to Him, He would be nailed to the cross with spikes instead of the usual manner of being tied with ropes.

Condemned men were obliged to carry their own crosses to the place of execution. Jesus did not permit Himself to be an exception. The heavy cross was placed on His shoulders and the Divine Master began the painful walk to Calvary. Before that day, death on a cross had been despised as the most terrible of humiliations. Jesus changed that image. From the first Good Friday onward, the cross has become a symbol of love.

61

Jesus patiently bore His cross to teach us a valuable lesson. He showed us that crosses are not just made of wood. Crosses can also be the events, circumstances or people that make up our everyday life. The challenge lies first in recognizing that cross, and second, in "carrying" it with all our hearts.

Journey in suffering

Wearied by the bloody sweat of Holy Thursday night in the garden called Gethsemane, tortured by the severe beating and the cruel crowning with thorns, exhausted because of lack of food and water, Jesus fell three times along the way to Calvary.

Three times He felt the parched roadway against His cheek. Each time the Master crawled to His knees, then to His feet and stumbled on.

Think about it

Jesus taught us that no matter how hard the road, or how weak we sometimes feel, we must never give in to the temptation to sin. We never again want to take the easy way of self-indulgence and self-centeredness.

Jesus meets His mother

In the midst of His pain and terrible humiliation, Jesus met His Mother. Their eyes exchanged tortured glances. Jesus saw all that His Mother was suffering and this caused new sorrow for Him. Mary's heart was breaking, and yet she understood that all of this had a deep meaning and infinite value. She realized the worth of every individual human being because she saw the price her Son was paying to save us from sin and an eternity without God.

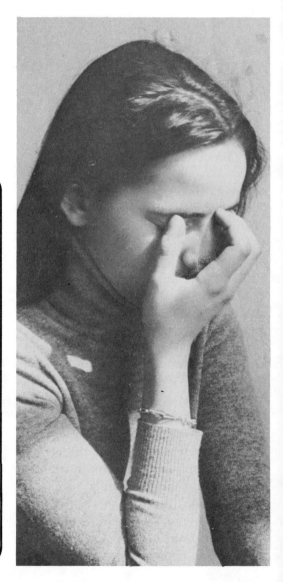

Simon of Cyrene

The soldiers realized that Jesus could no longer carry the cross alone. They forced a passerby named Simon of Cyrene to help Him. At first, Simon, a stranger, was resentful and embarrassed. He had not done anything to deserve a share in the Master's punishment and yet, the soldiers insisted that he help. As the man from Cyrene studied the crucified Christ, his anger melted. Slowly he became resigned, then eager to assist. He wanted to carry the entire load to spare Jesus that added suffering. The big, muscular stranger balanced the cross beam over his shoulders and started down the road. Strangely enough, it has been said that as Simon's attitude changed, as his reluctance turned to willingness, the cross seemed to grow lighter.

Before Jesus was to reach Calvary, the sorrowful women were to offer their consolation and tears and gentle Veronica would wipe His face with a soft clean cloth.

Think about it

When we shoulder our physical and spiritual crosses with fortitude and good will, our whole attitude becomes "super" natural. Sometimes our cross can be to obey those whom we should or to avoid certain friends and situations. It might be hard at first but the cross will grow light when our attitude becomes worthy of a follower of Jesus.

Evidence of Jesus in my life

To be a follower of Jesus calls for renunciation of my whims, weaknesses and sinful tendencies and habits. To overcome them, I rely on the strength that comes from Jesus. He will help me right now and every day as long as I never tire of asking Him.

Prayer

O Jesus, help me to remember throughout my life that when crosses come I should look to You. Give me the courage to carry each cross with self-sacrifice and courage. Often I look for the easy way out. This is to play the coward's role, and I will never find Your footsteps along such a path. Only You, Lord, can make me strong and self-sacrificing. Amen.

The Crucifixion

The sad procession moved down the road. The soldiers' whips prodded the condemned along. Jesus followed Simon of Cyrene closely as the big stranger carried the cross beam meant for the Son of God. Simon's face glowed with a new-found compassion as the realization of the tragedy unfolded. Finally, they arrived at Calvary.

Two thieves were also being crucified, but they were tied to their crosses. Jesus was not so blessed. Large spikes were driven into His wrists and feet as Mary, His Mother, looked on. She felt every bit of the pain and agony. The cross was slowly raised up and then dropped into a hole that had been dug for it.

The Savior hung for three long hours and while this sacred sacrifice was being fulfilled, people reacted in different ways. Some mocked Him still: "He saved others; let him save himself if he is the Christ of God, his chosen one" (Luke 23:35). The soldiers made fun of Him, too (see: Luke 23:37), and threw dice to see who would get His clothing. But Jesus, who could have called legions of angels to save Him, hung in quiet agony. Not a word, not even a gesture of resentment escaped Him.

A God and a thief

Time passed slowly and the suffering Christ, thirsty and tormented, prayed for His crucifiers.

"Father, forgive them," He said, "for they know not what they do" (Luke 23:34).

How different were the other two condemned men. They hung, one on each side of the Master. "Are you not the Christ?" asked the first. Contempt marked every word of his question. "Save yourself and us," he taunted (see: Luke 23:39). But the other man, guilty too of an evil life, a convicted thief like his companion, had a totally different reaction. Tradition gives him the name of *Dismas*.

Dismas' whole life flashed before his eyes. Days and weeks and months and years of sin taunted him. How could he possibly think that he, a common thief, would find salvation! No doubt he had never even thought about it until he hung next to the Master on the cross. For once in his life, he must have thought to himself, I'm going to do something right! He rebuked the other thief with an act of humility:

"Do you not fear God, since you are under the same sentence of condemnation? And we indeed justly; for we are receiving the due reward

66

for our deeds; but this man has done nothing wrong" (Luke 23:40-41).

Such a valiant and truthful statement opened the way for grace to enter Dismas' soul. "Jesus," he heard himself saying, "remember me when you come in your kingly power" (Luke 23:42). The tortured head of the Master turned until their eyes met—the eyes of a God and the eyes of a thief. Dismas became eager and confident. He listened for the words that would mean his salvation. Painfully those words did come forth from the lips of the world's Savior. Jesus replied:

"Truly I say to you, today you will be with me in Paradise."

(Luke 23:43)

Think about it

The challenge of the living of every day lies in our ability to apply the lessons the Divine Master taught with His life. He taught humility and lived it even when He was dying. He taught forgiveness and thoughtfulness and lived it even when He was dying. Whenever we meditate and pray in front of a crucifix, we can learn that lesson for ourselves.

His Mother was there

Mary, at the foot of her Son's cross, was comforted by the Apostle John (see: John 19:25-27). She was present in the joyful and the sad moments of her divine Son's life. She was there at Calvary to share His suffering and shame. She was the Mother of the Redeemer and she is our mother, too.

His mother heard Jesus utter a loud cry and give up His spirit to His Father (see: Luke 23:46). She stood looking up at Him as darkness covered the whole area and the curtain in the sanctuary of the temple split in two (see: Luke 23:44). He was dead, but before being taken down from the cross, a lance was thrust into His heart (see: John 19:34). And the sacrifice of Calvary was complete.

67

Think about it

We can never imagine what Jesus endured to save us or the suffering in His Mother's heart. The benefits of Jesus' suffering and dying are brought into our lives in every Mass or Eucharistic Celebration. The priest, acting in the Person of Christ, renews, in an unbloody manner, the most perfect sacrifice, Jesus' sacrifice of Calvary.

Evidence of Jesus in my life

Each time I see a crucifix I will remind myself that Jesus suffered the maximum, yet His concern is to carry my little troubles in His infinite heart. No more moodiness or self-centered thoughts for me!

Prayer

Divine Teacher, help me to grow in appreciation for the great treasure of the Mass. Many times, maybe even most of the time, I have taken my Catholic Faith for granted. But after studying about the events of Your passion and death, and realizing what Your infinite love for me cost You, Lord, I want to make You always "first" in my life. Amen.

Gift of the Spirit

In the New Testament we find:
- Jesus' promise to send the Holy Spirit
- the Holy Spirit working in the Church
- the Holy Spirit working in our souls
- the Holy Spirit bringing the divine life of grace
- the Holy Spirit bringing the theological and cardinal virtues as well as His Gifts and Fruits

Promise Fulfilled...

On Holy Thursday evening, at the Last Supper, Jesus gathered His Apostles around Him and told them many truths, mysterious and divine. Jesus knew He would suffer, die and rise again. He preached with great meaning to that small band whom He had chosen to carry His Church to the ends of the earth. But Peter and the other Apostles seemed perplexed. Jesus said to them:

"When I go and prepare a place for you, I will come again and will take you to myself, that where I am you may be also. And you know the way where I am going."

(John 14:3-4)

The Apostles listened and those words pierced the air and penetrated their souls, but the meaning remained obscure. Philip solved the riddle. "Lord," he asked bluntly, "show us the Father and we shall be satisfied" (John 14:8). But Jesus had a ready answer: "He who has seen me has seen the Father" (John 14:9). As Jesus explained further about the workings of divinity, He must have noticed the furrowed brows of His Apostles who were trying to understand divine mysteries, yet were having a hard time. And the merciful heart of the Savior reached out to each of them.

Sometimes a parent going on a trip tells his child, "I have to go away for a while, but when I come back, I'll bring home a gift just for you." In a way, during that Last Supper celebration, Jesus did that to His Apostles. He talked about His going back to the Father. And when this would happen, what would He do for the followers He had left behind? Jesus said:

"I will pray the Father,
and he will give you another
   Counselor,
to be with you forever..."

(John 14:16)

Have you ever noticed the techniques of a really good teacher? A good teacher repeats important points of the lesson more than once. To explain something twice for emphasis is to convince the students of the importance of that particular part of the message.

Jesus is the greatest Teacher who ever lived. Imagine the Divine Master in the Upper Room on that Holy Thursday evening. He wanted to emphasize the important things. One of the most important truths was His promise of the coming of the Holy Spirit. The Divine Teacher brought up the subject again:

"These things I have spoken to you, while I am still with you. But the Counselor, the Holy Spirit, whom the Father will send in my name, he will teach you all things, and bring to your remembrance all that I have said to you."

(John 14:25-26)

Two more times during that touching Last Supper homily, Jesus spoke of the Spirit (see: John 15:26; 16:7ff.).

Think about it

Oftentimes, we can find it so easy to drift along each day, taking many things for granted. Spiritual goals and spiritual duties like prayer have little appeal. We might notice, too, that we are so easily inclined to what we can see, feel, taste, hear and smell, in other words, to what our senses can grasp. But there is so much more to life than merely the "physical." There is so much more to each of us than merely the "physical." Who can help us to understand this more clearly? Who can help us to penetrate this truth more deeply? God the Holy Spirit can!

Who is the Holy Spirit?

The Holy Spirit, the Spirit of Truth, promised by the Divine Teacher, is the Third Person of the Blessed Trinity. He is God, as are the Father and the Son.

Some other names for the Holy Spirit are: Spirit of God, Gift of God, Spirit of Truth, Counselor and Paraclete. Paraclete means: "someone called upon for help." The term is especially used in relationship to a court of law. Jesus explained to the Apostles that the Holy Spirit, the Paraclete, would prosecute the world:

"When he (the Paraclete) comes, he will convince the world of sin and of righteousness and of judgment."

(John 16:8)

Think about it

Jesus wanted us to understand that those who truly follow Him cannot rightly live by the standards of the world. If God's life of grace is in us, then the Holy Spirit can work in and through us. If we put God first, then we live by His rules, the Ten Commandments, and our faith will grow. But Jesus knew how difficult this growing in faith would be, so He sent us the Paraclete, "someone called upon for help."

Evidence of Jesus in my life

If I think seriously about Jesus' standards and the world's standards, I begin to understand that Jesus expects diligence and exactness in doing my duties. Carelessness has no place in the life of Jesus' followers.

Prayer

Divine Holy Spirit, I believe in You.
I believe that You are God
and that You are the Paraclete
who will be with me as I live each day.
I want to be close to Jesus,
but I am weak.
Remind me often of what is right.
Strengthen me to follow what is right.
Help me to overcome the weak part of me.
Spirit of Truth, make me truthful with myself
so that I may admit how much I need You.

What Does the Holy Spirit Do for the Church?

The Holy Spirit is God. When we talk about what the Spirit does for us, we first think about Who He is. Because the Holy Spirit is God, He can do everything. He is the life, the breath, the soul of God's people, the Church. He lives in the Church and guides the Church. He also lives in each baptized person who has not driven Him out by serious or mortal sin.

Flames of fire

As we saw in the previous chapter, Jesus promised at the Last Supper to send His Spirit. As the Lord ascended into heaven, He left His Apostles and first group of followers with these words:

"Stay in the city, until you are clothed with power from on high" (Luke 24:49).

The power from on high...what would it be? How would it manifest itself? How would that power be recognized? All of these questions are easily answered by St. Luke in the Acts of the Apostles, chapter two:

"When the day of Pentecost had come, they were all together in one place. And suddenly a sound came from heaven like the rush of a mighty wind, and it filled all the house where they were sitting. And there appeared to them tongues as of fire, distributed and resting on each one of them. And they were all filled with the Holy Spirit and began to speak in other tongues, as the Spirit gave them utterance.

"Now there were dwelling in Jerusalem Jews, devout men from every nation under heaven. And at this sound the multitude came together, and they were bewildered, because each one heard them speaking in his own language. And they were amazed and wondered, saying, 'Are not all these who are speaking Galileans? And how is it that we hear, each of us in his own native language? Parthians and Medes and Elamites and residents of Mesopotamia, Judea and Cappadocia, Pontus and Asia, Phrygia and Pamphylia, Egypt and the parts of Libya belonging to Cyrene, and visitors from Rome, both Jews and proselytes, Cretans and Arabians, we hear them telling in our own tongues the mighty works of God'" (Acts 2:1-11).

Think about it

Does the Holy Spirit have power? Is He powerful? Just reflect on what He did for Peter and the first Apostles. Until Pentecost, and the descent of the Holy Spirit, the Apostles had been fearful, bewildered, powerless. They left their locked Upper Room and went outside to preach to the Jerusalem crowds. That famous Pentecost has been called the *birthday of the Church*. The Holy Spirit gave the Apostles the courage to proclaim the Good News in public. And what were the results? St. Luke explains:

"So those who received his word were baptized; and there were added that day about three thousand souls."

(Acts 2:41)

The Holy Spirit in the Pope and bishops

Nearly two thousand years have passed since that Pentecost when the Holy Spirit came down in the form of tongues of fire on the first Pope, St. Peter, and the Apostles, the first bishops. And even though the Spirit does not usually choose in our day such dynamic outward manifestations as He did on that Pentecost, He joins God's people, the Church, in faith and love. He guides the Church's chief teachers, the Pope and bishops united to the Pope, so that they will not make mistakes when they teach us what to believe and how to live.

Although the Holy Spirit was active in the world before Jesus' resurrection, we think of Pentecost as the day when He first made Himself known to Jesus' followers. He gave the Apostles courage to manifest all that Jesus had taught them by His life and teaching. The Paraclete gave them a deeper understanding of those teachings. He also gave them grace, a spirit of sacrifice, and joined them more closely together.

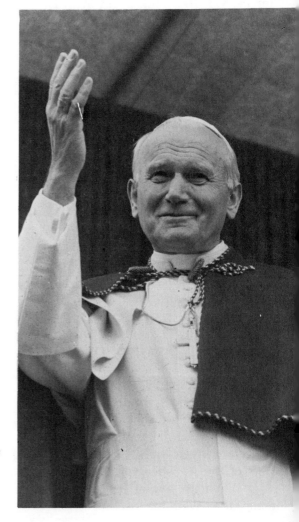

The Holy Spirit does the very same for the Pope and bishops today. He gives them courage to proclaim Christ's message to the people. The Pope is responsible for all the Catholics in the world. Each bishop is responsible for those Catholics in his diocese.

Frequently, the Pope and bishops find it necessary to stand up for Christ so as to protect His people from false doctrines, error, suggestions to sin, oppression and falling into totally secular life styles.

Church leaders pray for guidance, for courage and a deeper understanding of the truths that God has revealed. Through prayer, the Holy Spirit comes to the Pope and bishops and fills them with divine consolation and strength to lead God's people through this often trouble-filled life to eternal life with God in heaven.

In the Acts of the Apostles, we read that Peter and John were told not to preach about Jesus, but they proclaimed Him just the same.

Think about it

There is no other human being alive today who has had more of an impact on the whole world than Pope John Paul II. He has been seen by more people throughout the world than any other human being who ever lived. In his numerous world trips, he meets people who love him, who cherish his presence as if he were Jesus Himself. The Pope also meets those who criticize him, insult him, shun the Gospel message and despise the Church he represents. Still the Pope courageously proclaims all the doctrinal content of the Catholic Faith that comes from Christ Himself. He says with the Apostles Peter and John:

"For we cannot but speak of what we have seen and heard" (Acts 4:20).

Pope John Paul receives that courage from the Holy Spirit.

Evidence of Jesus in my life

I can live my life in an easy-going way, wasting time. Or I can make each moment count for God by doing each duty as well as I am able. I can begin now by using the present moment well.

Prayer

Come mighty Spirit into my soul. Give me at least some of the love and appreciation for my Catholic Faith that Pope John Paul II has.

Help me to take heart and to have patience with myself who am so easily impatient when it comes to spiritual things.

Help me to want to pray, and inspire me to ask—not for what I want but for what I need—to become a fervent follower of Jesus.

The Holy Spirit in Us!

Blind Bartimaeus

A crowd had gathered along both sides of the road that led to Jericho. They watched and waited as the hot sun beat down. No one was about to leave. Jesus of Nazareth was worth the wait. Some were there out of curiosity. Others sought a Savior and hoped it would be He.

Suddenly, He was there, surrounded by His little band called Apostles. There was shouting fused with whispering and exclamations of joy. A man sat by the side of the road. He could feel the excitement of the crowd. He knew who was coming; he had heard the name so often. If only he could make himself visible to the One who could help him. The crowd drew nearer and nearer. They seemed to be in front of the blind man. His eyes could not see, but his lungs were powerful enough. Bartimaeus called out: "Jesus, Son of David, have pity on me!" (Mark 10:47). Several people tried rudely to silence him, but Bartimaeus ignored them and called even louder: "Son of David, have pity on me!" (Mark 10:48)

Even with the commotion of the crowd, Jesus heard that cry for help. He felt the plea. Jesus stopped, looked toward the blind man and said: "Call him over." Jesus' disciples reassured the blind man: "You have nothing to fear from him! Get up! He is calling you!" That was an invitation Bartimaeus was not going to pass up. It was not everyday that a man had the opportunity to grow closer to Jesus. "Bartimaeus jumped up and went to stand in front of Jesus" (Mark 10:50).

The blind man stood there smiling and hopeful. Somehow he could tell that Jesus was smiling, too. The noise of the crowd died down. Silence set in. Then even though Jesus knew the answer, He asked: "What do you want me to do for you?" (Mark 10:50). The man did not mince words. "Master," he said, "let me receive my sight" (Mark 10:52). While the crowd watched in silence, the Master replied: "Go your way; your faith has made you well" (Mark 10:52).

Bartimaeus was instantly cured of his blindness. He could clearly see people and the world around him for the first time in his entire life. Mark concludes the short event with: "Immediately he received his sight and followed him on the way" (Mark 10:52).

Jesus had said: "Go your way," but Bartimaeus followed Him up the road. The blind man had received more than a physical gift from Jesus. He had received the gift of great trust in God.

Think about it

Bartimaeus lived a long time ago, but he teaches a lesson to us. We, too, receive many spiritual gifts from the Divine Teacher through the Holy Spirit. Do we recognize the gifts and follow Jesus "up the road" of life?

Recognizing Him...

The first Christians recognized the presence of the Holy Spirit in the mighty wind and tongues of fire. Today His presence is usually not so dramatic but is equally effective. Just because we do not see a hovering dove or flames or hear vibrant wind, the Holy Spirit is there with us and in us. The challenge for each of us is to let Him work in our lives.

His special gift

The special gift that the Holy Spirit gives us is grace which was won for us by Jesus' death on the cross. Just as we cannot see the Holy Spirit with our human eyes, so we cannot see grace, but grace is as real as the Holy Spirit is real.

Grace is God's life in us, a special gift He freely gives us that we may share in His happiness. Grace means "loving favor." God's grace is supernatural, that is, "above the powers of any creature." Grace brings us close to God. Grace was given to each of us when we were baptized. We can make grace grow in us through prayer and by receiving the sacraments of Eucharist and Reconciliation well. Grace gives us strength and help to live as Christ wants.

What grace is and does

There are different kinds of grace because we need many kinds of help from God, and He is generous in giving help. The state of grace is a sharing in God's own life, a state of friendship with Him. This "sharing in God's own life" may also be called sanctifying grace, which means a divine gift that makes us holy. This grace is necessary for sharing in God's life and happiness after death.

It is important to learn about grace, because this gift can be lost if we are not on our guard. Mortal sin can drive sanctifying grace from our souls. Who could be so ungrateful, so careless or callous as to throw away the treasure of grace? The Holy Spirit and sin cannot dwell together.

Instant help

When we are tempted to sin, what can we do? We can pray.... We can ask the Lord for help. When we ask, we receive actual graces. Actual graces are temporary and immediate helps from the Holy Spirit which make us able to know and do what God expects of us at a certain moment. Actual grace may also be described as a temporary light for the mind or strength for the will by which God helps us to avoid sin or to do something good. The treasure of actual graces is at our disposal no matter how weak we are, no matter how little good we have done or how often we have failed to ask for God's help.

Think about it

God gives actual graces to everyone. Actual graces, quick spiritual helps, are ours for the asking. Actual graces are different from the virtues and gifts which we will talk about later. Actual graces are temporary, whereas the virtues and gifts are "permanent" in the soul. (In fact, some of the virtues remain even when grace has been driven from the soul by mortal sin.) Actual graces do not force us to do what is right because God leaves us free, but they are powerful if we cooperate with them.

Evidence of Jesus in my life

God touched Bartimaeus' life in a unique way. He transformed the twelve Apostles, too. Do I try to notice His presence in my everyday life? Am I willing to make more of an effort to think and live in His presence always?

Prayer

Come, mighty Spirit, You who are God;
work in my soul. Remind me of how much
I need God's help. Remind me, too, of the
gift of grace that is mine for the asking.
I pray so little and when I neglect prayer,
I deprive myself of the help I need to
journey through this life in such a way
that it becomes a preparation for heaven.
I need You, mighty Spirit, to transform my life.

God-Centered Virtues

Run the race to win

When we study about our Catholic Faith, it should not seem unusual to learn new terminology or to find that some ordinary words have "religious" definitions. Religious terminology is important to learn and be familiar with. One such term is "merit." "Merit" is the "right" to a reward in heaven. Merits are earned by those who have God's grace and pray or do good works for love of Him.

The doctrine or belief about "merit" helps us to understand the divine psychology of a loving God. He made us to share in His eternal homeland, heaven. Heaven is not our right, but a gift. Heaven is so precious a gift that the Creator wants us to earn the gift, to "pay" for the gift, as much as is possible, with our poor human good actions performed out of love for Him. St. Paul was very much aware of making everything in his life "count for Christ." He said:

"I do it all for the sake of the gospel, that I may share in its blessings" (1 Corinthians 9:23).

The people of Corinth, one of the communities to whom Paul wrote, were sports-minded people. To them nothing was as important as winning. Paul wanted to impress spiritual values on them, so he went to the trouble of relating Gospel ideals to something they were interested in: good sportsmanship.

"Do you not know that in a race all the runners compete, but only one receives the prize? So run that you may obtain it."

(1 Corinthians 9:24)

How to grow in virtue

A "virtue" is a power to do good or a habit of doing good. The main virtues that God gives us are the:

theological virtues (God-centered)

cardinal virtues (hinge or key)— also called moral virtues.

Although these virtues are free gifts of God, we must use them, so that they truly become the habits of doing good that God meant them to be.

When a person is canonized a saint, the Pope explains that the new saint was, while he or she lived on this earth, exemplary in the practice of the theological and cardinal virtues.

The theological virtues are God-given and God-centered habits of doing good. They are: faith, hope and charity. By the word "theological" is meant: that which pertains to God.

Faith, hope and love

Faith is the virtue by which we believe in God and everything He has taught us. The Bible is full of examples of those who had faith, or the beginning of faith, in God. When Lazarus, the brother of Martha and Mary, had died, Jesus said to Martha:

"I am the resurrection and the
    life;
he who believes in me,
though he die, yet shall he live,
and whoever lives and believes
in me shall never die."

(John 11:25)

We exercise the virtue of faith when we recite the Creed at Mass, the Apostles Creed and the Act of Faith meaning the words as we say them. We exercise faith when we believe wholeheartedly all the truths taught by the teaching authority of the Catholic Church. We exercise faith every time we make the Sign of the Cross.

Hope is the virtue by which we trust that our all-powerful and faithful God will bring us to heaven if we live as He asks us to live. We nourish in our hearts hope for eternal life with God when we tell God often that we trust in His infinite goodness, and His personal care for each of us. How important we are to God, not because of our intelligence or talents, but because we are His creatures. Jesus said:

"Look at the birds of the air; they neither sow nor reap nor gather into barns and yet your heavenly Father feeds them. Are you not of more value than they?" (Matthew 6:26)

When we think often about God's personal love for each of us, we stop being anxious; we stop worrying about little or even big things. We think of ourselves as small creatures in the palm of God's all-powerful hand and we hope in His continuing care. Even when we feel alone or unloved, disappointed or sad, we have reason to be at peace. God loves each of us and He has promised us heaven.

Charity is the virtue by which we love God above everything else and love all other people for His sake. We manifest our love for God when we obey the Ten Commandments and believe and practice sincerely what the Church teaches. We also show our love by acts of service done for love of Jesus. Jesus said:

"So whatever you wish that men would do to you, do so to them; for this is the law and the prophets" (Matthew 7:12).

Unselfish, generous love grows in our heart when we make acts of Love especially when receiving Jesus in Holy Communion.

Think about it

Being a Christian, and in particular, a Catholic Christian, we begin to reflect more deeply on our obligation to grow in the spiritual life and to practice the virtues of faith, hope and charity. To grow in the spiritual life is not a burden, but a source of great joy and peace. It is a new-found dimension of our lives lived for God. Perhaps, until today, we have never even thought about this. But now, as we prepare to receive the Holy Spirit in the sacrament of Confirmation, we are more aware of our duties, and opportunities for growth in God's life. We ask the Divine Teacher to make us more mature in accepting our spiritual responsibilities.

Evidence of Jesus in my life

"Love" is the mark of the Christian. How do I treat those with whom I live or associate? Do I examine myself frequently on my thoughts, words, attitudes? When tempted to be mean or revengeful, do I try to replace these thoughts with the words and actions of Jesus?

Prayer

Divine Teacher, once Your first Pope, St. Peter, wrote to the early Christians: "Without having seen him you love him; though you do not now see him you believe in him and rejoice with unutterable and exalted joy" (1 Peter 1:8). Belief is faith; hope is trust and love is charity for You and all people near and far because they belong to You. May Your Holy Spirit fill my soul with these God-centered virtues and may I become, with His and Your help, what I should.

Growing in the Spirit's Life

Growing close to God and remaining close to Him is the result of grace, the gift of His life in us. We have seen in the previous lesson that God the Holy Spirit infuses in our hearts the three theological virtues of faith, hope and charity. These are God-centered habits that grow as we exercise them.

These three gifts are so wonderful that it seems impossible that the Holy Spirit could bring us still more. But He does. He infuses in us the cardinal virtues.

These are also called the *moral* virtues because they form a basis on which all the other virtues about right living depend.

The cardinal or hinge virtues are: prudence, justice, fortitude and temperance. The power to practice each of these virtues comes from the Holy Spirit's gift of grace.

Prudence

Prudence is the virtue by which a person puts heaven before everything else. He or she thinks carefully before acting, makes wise choices, and does things well. Looking at this definition, we can ask ourselves: what does it mean for me to put heaven before everything else? It means to form the habit of remembering often the reason why God gave me life on this earth. With my goal in mind, I think out my will choices, saying "no" to what is wrong and saying "yes" to what I should be doing.

A prudent person does things well. Diligence is part of this "hinge" virtue. Aware of the importance of prudence, I ask the Holy Spirit to help me evaluate the way I live my life. I ask the Holy Spirit to help me see how I take my responsibilities at

whom we, in any way, come in contact. We will talk more about justice under the commandments.

Fortitude

Fortitude is the virtue by which a person does what is good and right in spite of any difficulty. Fortitude is the hero's virtue. People who practice this virtue are true to their faith in Christ even if they have to suffer something. Those brave followers of Christ who have been persecuted for remaining true to Him practice the virtue of fortitude when they refuse to give up their Catholic Faith. Some, down through the centuries, like the first Pope, St. Peter, and the great Apostle, St. Paul, died rather than give up their faith in Christ. Those who give up their life for their Catholic Faith are martyrs.

Temperance

Temperance is the virtue by which a person exercises self-control with regard to the drives or urges of human nature. The person who practices the virtue of temperance does not over-indulge in food and drink. The temperate person is regulated in his personal life. He learns how to say "no" to the cravings of his human nature that oppose God's laws. For example: an unmarried person who keeps his or her sexual instincts in check because of his or her love for Christ, practices the virtue of temperance. Such a person cultivates purity in thoughts, words and actions in imitation of Jesus, Mary and the saints who practiced the virtue of purity. We will meet the virtue of purity again in our study of the sixth and ninth commandments.

home and at school. I might have to admit honestly that I will have to correct some things that are not right. But there is nothing to fear. The Holy Spirit will give His grace to become better.

Justice

Justice is the virtue by which a person is fair to everyone, first of all, to God. Being fair to God might sound strange at first. But being fair to God means acknowledging that God is God and that we are His creatures. Part of being fair to God, for example, is by worshiping Him at the Eucharistic Celebration every Sunday (or Saturday evening, if we cannot go to Mass on Sunday because of travel, work, or another good reason). Being just with people means thinking, speaking and acting rightly with every human being with

The gifts of the Holy Spirit

What else does the Spirit bring? Laden with still more spiritual delights, the Holy Spirit brings us His gifts and fruits. The gifts of the Holy Spirit are seven special inclinations that the Spirit gives us so that we will be more ready and willing to do what He expects of us. The gifts of the Holy Spirit prepare us to receive actual graces and make it easier to practice the virtues.

The gifts of the Holy Spirit are wisdom, understanding, right judgment (or counsel), courage (or fortitude), knowledge, reverent love (or piety) and holy fear.

Wisdom is the gift which helps us to love spiritual things, to put God in the first place in our lives, and to judge everything either as a help or as an obstacle to reaching heaven.

The gift of *understanding* helps us to see more deeply into the truths we already believe by faith.

Right judgment helps us to choose what is right, even in difficult circumstances.

Courage is the gift which helps us to be brave and patient in overcoming difficulties and carrying out our duties.

Knowledge is the gift which helps us to know God and what He expects of us through what He has created.

Reverent love helps us to love God as our Father and all people. When we practice this gift, we serve God as He deserves and our brothers and sisters in Him.

Holy fear helps us to respect God and to want to please Him in everything.

The fruits of the Holy Spirit

The fruits of the Holy Spirit are good deeds and habits that result from our response to the Holy Spirit's inspirations to do good (actual graces). The gifts are: charity, joy, peace, patience, kindness, goodness, longsuffering, humility, fidelity, modesty, continence, chastity.

Think about it

When the Holy Spirit comes into our lives, He brings a spiritual banquet we never imagined. All He asks is that we cooperate with His inspirations. It does us good to study about the virtues, gifts and fruits that the Third Person of the Blessed Trinity brings us because we realize that when we think a holy thought, when we say a good word or perform a good action, the Holy Spirit inspired that good thought, word or action. This helps us to strive to be humble. Humility, in fact, is the virtue by which we truly know ourselves and see that whatever is good in us comes from God.

Evidence of Jesus in my life

As a Christian and a Catholic, I am called by the Lord to practice the virtues I have been studying about. If I take a blank piece of paper and try to make a list, how many virtues of mine can I write down?

Prayer

Come Holy Spirit into my soul.
Make the virtues You so generously gave me at Baptism
take root anew and grow in me.
Help me especially in the virtues You know I need most.
Up until now I have given so little
importance to Your life in me,
but now all that is changed.
Help me to cooperate with Your work
to make me a better person.
Fill me with Your gifts and fruits
and be free to work in me.

The Church Jesus Gave Us

- Jesus' Church spreads beyond Palestine.

- Through the Pope, the Successor of St. Peter, the Church teaches and guides us.

- In union with the Pope, the bishops, as successors of the Apostles, continue Jesus' saving mission.

- The Church Jesus left us can be recognized by four distinguishing marks.

- The Church's Mother and Queen is Mary, Jesus' own Mother.

Beyond All Boundaries

The boat docked at Puteoli (see: Acts 28:13), and the veteran missionary disembarked. Chains hung from his wrists and a Roman centurion was at his side. The man in chains was short, a little bent, plain-looking and fatherly. Years of prayer had mellowed his forceful temperament into a quiet, eloquent strength. He was no criminal, this man in chains, nor was he ordinary.

Roman Christians who had heard of his arrival walked a day's journey and more to meet him and accompany him to the city of Rome. The man looked at that group of believers. He read in their faces their joy at finding faith in Christ. Somehow his years of traveling with the hardships of shipwreck, privations, beatings, prison terms, insults—seemed worth it all. The infant Church was indeed growing. It had even penetrated Imperial Rome. These Christians lining the sleek Roman road were living proof.

Paul of Tarsus, known for all time as the Apostle of the Nations, "thanked God and took fresh courage" (Acts 28:15). As he entered Rome, Paul's fourth missionary journey ended. He was to live under house arrest for two years before his case would be tried by the Emperor Nero. But those days, weeks, months and years of waiting would be filled to capacity because Paul preached Christ's Gospel to all who came to him.

What was the driving power behind St. Paul? What was the motivating force? The power and force behind St. Paul was none other than Jesus, God and man. Paul was totally familiar with the truths of salvation that Christ revealed. Therefore, he loved Jesus and all that He taught and the Church He founded.

Why the Church?

The Church that Paul loved and taught about is the Church that we are members of, the Church founded by Jesus Himself. Jesus started His Church to continue His mission of bringing all people to eternal salvation. He told the eleven Apostles to proclaim His message to everybody (see: Mark 16:15-16).

If you were coming to know the Catholic Church for the first time, how could you recognize her as the true Church? The Catholic Church, the true Church founded by Jesus Christ, can be known by these characteristics together:

These Christians profess loyalty to the Pope and bishops joined with him.

There is oneness in the truths to be believed and the moral code to be followed.

There is oneness in worship: the sacrifice of the Mass, and the means to holiness, the seven sacraments.

In future lessons, we will look at these characteristics of the true Church more closely.

A Catholic is a member of the Roman Catholic Church, which is distinguished from all other Christian churches by its loyalty to the Pope, who is the head of Jesus' Church because he is the successor of St. Peter. The earnest Catholic accepts what the Church teaches as coming from Christ Himself, and strives to conform his or her life to those teachings.

Think about it

Jesus, the Son of God, walked this earth for some thirty-three years. He gave us the doctrine to be believed, the truths of Faith to cherish. He proposed Himself as the Truth. In fact, He is the only one who could ever say: "I am the Truth."

While He was with us in His human nature, He showed us how to live. He proclaimed the loftiest moral code the world has ever known as the way to heaven. He gave us Himself to be our Way. In fact, He is the only one who could ever say: "I am the Way."

Because He is God and knows our weak human nature totally, Jesus realized that we could never believe His lofty teachings or be true to His high moral values without the help of grace which is life. He gave Himself to us as our Life. In fact, Jesus is the only one who could ever say: "I am the life."

In that definition of Himself: "I am the way, and the truth, and the life" (John 14:6), Jesus showed us the way to heaven.

But that was not all. To insure that His true doctrine, moral guidelines and means of grace be continued for all people of all times, Jesus left us His Church and sent the Holy Spirit to remain with the Church and her faithful members always.

Evidence of Jesus in my life

Someone once said: "Don't just keep the Faith. Spread it!" What have I done this past week to be a witness for Christ to those around me?

Prayer

Jesus, Divine Teacher, in Your great love,
You thought of everything.
You left us Your Church with Your living message of salvation.
You left us the Holy Spirit to work in our hearts.
You left us truths to fill our minds, examples to follow
and the sacraments to give us Your life of grace.
What I need, in all honesty,
is a new awareness of what I have been given.
What I need is a love for the Faith, a love for the Church.
Help me to love the Church as St. Paul loved her
and to become a real follower of Yours.

The Church Teaches Still

Jesus started His Church to continue His mission of bringing all people to eternal salvation. In order to do that, the Church has to be a Teacher. The Church has to voice what we are to believe and how we are to live. The Church has to voice the practices, customs and devotions by which Catholics express their Faith.

The Holy Spirit's special role in the Church is to keep its members faithful to Jesus' teachings until the end of time. The Holy Spirit also helps the Church to constantly become holier and better in the Church itself and in its members.

Jesus remains with us still in His Church. He is teaching us about the truths that lead to eternal life. He is teaching us the moral values that guide us along the road to holiness and union with God.

But all kinds of voices shout other messages. Each of those voices preaches as if his or her words were true. How can we ever decipher the authentic voice of Jesus the Teacher today almost two thousand years after He has returned to heaven? This wise Teacher—who is Wisdom Himself—has thought of an ingenious way to make Himself heard to all who will listen. Especially, He has given us the chief teacher in His Church, the Pope.

Peter the Rock

It was an afternoon in Caesarea Philippi. The twelve Apostles, gathered around Jesus, were discussing who the people thought He was. Most seemed to think that Jesus was a prophet. The Lord asked the Twelve: "But who do you say that I am?" Peter stepped forward, looked intently at His Master and said: "You are the Messiah, the Son of the living God." The answer was absolutely correct. The Lord showed His gratitude. He, the Founder of His Church, was about to make Peter His Vicar. In other words, Peter would be made the visible head of Jesus' Church to remain as teacher and leader of God's people after Jesus would return to the Father.

Think about it

Jesus started a Church that would be visible in the world until the end of time. Jesus said to Peter:

"And I tell you, you are Peter, and on this rock I will build my church, and the powers of death shall not prevail against it. I will give you the keys to the kingdom of heaven, and whatever you bind on earth shall be bound in heaven, and whatever you loose on earth shall be loosed in heaven."

(Matthew 16:18-19)

Peter was made the first Pope by Jesus Himself. But the office of Pope could not end with the death of St. Peter. What would happen to the members of Jesus' Church? Every Pope from St. Linus, the second Pope, to our present Pope John Paul II, is the Vicar of Christ and the chief teacher and leader of God's people just as St. Peter was. Jesus told Peter: "Feed my lambs" (John 21:15), and "Feed my sheep" (John 21:17). To the Pope, who takes the place of Jesus, the Good Shepherd, is entrusted the care of the whole Church.

Why the Pope is important

When a Pope is elected, he takes on a singular role and a heavy responsibility. Jesus, the Church's Founder, is entrusting to him the care of every member of His Church. The Pope takes the place of Jesus in the Church. The Catholic Church will always have a Pope because this is what Jesus wanted. The Pope is elected (after invoking the Holy Spirit), from among the group of bishops and archbishops called Cardinals. To remind himself and everyone of his responsibility as Chief Shepherd of the whole flock, the Pope chooses a new name. He may select the name of a saint or a preceding Pope, whose example of virtue will influence the spirit of the new Pope's reign.

The Pope—every Pope—is a gift from Jesus the Teacher to His people. Each Pope is uniquely himself, with his own personality, background, appearance, virtues, talents and insight.

The Pope is so important to the Church because He is the chief teacher and leader. He, as Christ's Vicar, holds the place of Jesus in the Church.

To love and cherish the Pope means to love and cherish Jesus Himself.

Think about it

Many people on the world scene, or even in our own lives, might try to steer our lives in one direction or another, but we can be tranquil because Jesus the Teacher has left us a sure, visible guide who is led by the Holy Spirit in teaching us what to believe and do in order to be saved. The Pope can say with Jesus:

"I am the good shepherd; and my own know me... and I lay down my life for the sheep" (John 10:14-15).

The Pope feels the responsibility for our souls. He holds the "first place" in teaching, governing and guiding Catholics in what they believe and how they live. Sometimes the Pope is called the "Prince of the Apostles," the title given to the first Pope. It means that he is the first among the Apostles; the leader of the group. The word "papal" means that which refers to the Pope. "Pontiff," in ordinary speech, is another name for Pope.

Safeguard

Jesus left His Church fully equipped to be the teacher par excellence. He spared nothing to keep her living and active in the world. The gift of infallibility is freedom from making a mistake when teaching a truth of faith or right living (morals). It comes from the Holy Spirit and is given in certain circumstances to the Pope and bishops united with him. Infallibility is a gift given for the good of the whole Church.

The term "ex cathedra" is Latin and means "from the chair" of St. Peter. It is used when referring to the Pope's infallible statements regarding what Catholics must believe and live.

Think about it

Infallibility does not mean impeccability or freedom from personal sin. Infallibility does not mean that the Pope can never make the slightest mistake or error in human judgment. Infallibility does mean that when the Pope officially proclaims a truth to be believed by all the people, through the divine help of the Holy Spirit, that truth is free from error and is what Jesus the Teacher proclaims.

What the Pope means to me

A Catholic woman explains: "I have to admit that in the 1960's I was not a very good advertisement for the Catholic Church. I did not go to Mass nor did I really care. In 1968, I turned 39. That same year the famous encyclical: *Humanae vitae* (Latin for *Of Human Life*) was issued by Pope Paul VI. In that document, artificial birth control was pronounced an immoral means of regulating births. Artificial contraception was declared to be directly against the law of God because it contradicts the purpose of marriage.

"But before that summer day when the Pope published the encyclical, predictions of what the Pope would say abounded. You know how it is...certain people have opinions on everything and if they talk long enough and loud enough, they have a solution for everything. Some of my friends were no different.

"One day after lunch, someone said: 'The decision from the Pope about the morality of birth control will soon come out. For sure, he'll side with the majority. Everyone does it.'

"Someone else added: 'Things are different today. The Church has to change or no one will go to church anymore.' And on and on they went. I sat silently and began to think. I looked around at the group. Several were Catholics. A few were even graduates of Catholic high schools and colleges. All had good jobs and all were married, except two. I wondered what the non-Catholics among us must have thought. And then I became curious about what the

Pope would *really* say. After all, the Pope is the Pope. He represents Christ who is God, and God does not change His mind. Just because *everyone* does it? Is God *democratic?* I did not really think so. And I decided to sit back, wait and see....

"On the famous day when the encyclical was published, that tiny seed of faith inside of me began to break open and grow again, that faith I had been smothering and starving by my failure to nourish it through participating at Mass and receiving the sacraments. It seemed to me that Pope Paul VI stood all alone defending the law of Christ. The media, the press, even some of those who should have been most faithful to the Vicar of Christ launched out against him. And yet he did not back down or change his message. That is when I decided, *'This is the Church I want to belong to'*—a Church that doesn't compromise or change its beliefs in the face of opposition.

"Since I made my decision, I have not missed daily Mass. I have deepened my faith by good reading, prayer and study. Although many years have gone by, I will always cherish the memory of Pope Paul VI who spoke and taught in the place of Christ so that we would know the way that leads to eternal life. Isn't that what really matters in the end?"

Evidence of Jesus in my life

Do I make it my personal responsibility to stand up for and defend the Pope whenever an opportunity presents itself? Do I pray daily that the Divine Teacher will bless and protect the Pope?

Prayer

I hear many uncertain trumpets, Lord.
But You left us the sure teacher and guide
in your Church—the Pope.
He has been given a great heart
to love all his people in every part of the world.
He loves us with a personal love,
as You do, Jesus.
Help me to listen to and believe the Pope.
Guide me to make the effort to read his words and obey him.
He points out the "sure way" to You.
Help me to always appreciate and love Your gift, the Pope.

Continuing Jesus' Work

The Divine Teacher was making it very clear that He would not be on earth forever or for long. He was already dropping hints about His future betrayal and death, a topic that put His Apostles on edge whenever He brought it up. Aside from that, it was quite certain that He was preparing men He Himself had chosen to carry on the work He had begun. In the first place, of course, this meant His twelve Apostles.

Anyone could tell there was something special about this closely-knit group. Jesus told them things in private which He did not tell the crowds at large. They spent almost all their time with Him, as full-time companions or students, and they knew this Teacher better than most did.

The first Apostles were to leave their mark on the early Church. Transformed by the Holy Spirit and motivated by a burning love for Jesus and His Church, the Apostles took that love to the various parts of the world. All died as martyrs, except the Apostle St. John, who lived to be over one hundred years old.

Jesus' Church was founded on men known as the Apostles. They would not live forever, so how was the Church to continue in time? Where would she receive the moral guidance to move on her sure course through time? With the death of the Apostles, was Jesus' Church, as He had founded it, to die, too?

Just as St. Peter's vital role as Christ's Vicar would continue in every Pope until the end of time, so the Apostles' successors are the bishops.

The men in the Church who continue the mission of the Apostles are the Pope, who is the chief bishop, and all the other bishops united with him. They lead in Jesus' name. The Pope and bishops considered together as the teaching authority in the Church are called the *Magisterium*. They are also called the *hierarchy*. To be a bishop is a great privilege and bears an equally great responsibility.

Bishops, with the Pope, are called to teach, rule and sanctify God's people. What do bishops teach? The bishops are heralds or messengers of the King whom they serve—Jesus Himself. They teach the truths that Jesus taught and they teach the moral values that Jesus taught and lived. They administer the sacraments. Bishops ordain bishops and they ordain men to the priesthood and diaconate as well.

Bishops lead and teach the Catholics of their dioceses. A diocese is a section of territory made up of parishes placed by the Pope under the care of a bishop or archbishop. Dioceses vary in sizes and number of parishes. More important dioceses are called archdioceses; their spiritual leader is called an archbishop.

Think about it

How much the early Christians revered Peter and the first Apostles. That core group, who were the Teaching Authority, was listened to, obeyed and loved.

The Church is much larger now and world-wide, yet, bishops, the successors of the Apostles, remain teachers. They bear the responsibility for the souls of their flock. That is why we want to be attentive to their teachings as the early Christians were to the Apostles. How wise to listen to the bishop of our diocese, to read his words in the diocesan newspaper, to be present, when possible, at some of the liturgies and ceremonies in which the bishop is present. When we make ourselves available to the bishop, we deepen our faith and our love for the Church.

Maintaining unity

Because He is God, Jesus the Teacher saw beyond His original Apostles to a Church world-wide, so closely united that it would be called His own body, His Mystical Body. When we call the Catholic Church Christ's Mystical Body, we mean the real union of members of the Church (living and deceased) with Jesus and one another, through the grace-giving activity of the Holy Spirit. This close-knit body founded by Jesus on Peter the Rock and the Apostles continues guiding all people to salvation through the Pope and the bishops.

Two expressions of the unity of Church leaders are: the *college of bishops* and the *college of Cardinals*. By the *college of bishops* is meant that all of the bishops throughout the world united with the Pope form one body called the hierarchy or apostolic college.

The *college of Cardinals* is the term used to mean all of the Cardinals as a united body. This body—chosen individually from among bishops and priests by the Pope to be his advisors—also elect a new Pope.

An ecumenical council is a meeting of the bishops of the whole world, called together by the Pope to discuss and explain Church teaching and to set forth guidelines for the People of God. With the Pope's approval, an ecumenical council's conclusions are to be accepted by all the faithful and put into practice.

Think about it

The Holy Spirit is the soul of the Church. A characteristic or sign of the presence of the Holy Spirit is unity. The bishops, as if one, collaborate with the Pope. The Cardinals help the Holy Father to carry his awesome burden of the welfare of the whole Church. The hierarchy's unity is a reflection of the unity found in the Blessed Trinity. The hierarchy's unity and harmony is a reflection of the unity we should foster at home, in the classroom, in the neighborhood and with whomever we come in contact.

Evidence of Jesus in my life

I live in a diocese, the chief teacher of which is the local bishop. Do I realize my obligation to pray often for him who shoulders a heavy burden for Jesus' Church?

Prayer

Jesus, Divine Teacher,
You have made Your Church visible—
a light for all to see and recognize.
Your Pope and bishops guide us in your name.
Give me love and respect for their presence.
Help me to heed their word and obey their teachings
even at the cost of personal sacrifice.
Give me the strength to listen to them as I would to You,
the Divine Teacher, and not to follow
after popular trends and easy prophets.
Help me to be a "sower" of unity
among all those around me.

How To Recognize Jesus' Church

Fishermen out on the open seas, looking for the catch that will be their livelihood, spend long days and nights tossed by the rhythmic motion of the boat. As the time drones on, and they become anxious to return to their homes and families, they are overjoyed when enough fish are caught and they can begin the long trip back to port.

Fishermen meet all kinds of weather: storms, clouds, fog and the rest. But as the waves toss their vessel, or as the fog engulfs them, they focus their glance on the distant shore...and know that it is there because of the rays from the lighthouse near the water's edge. How many times a ship steers into port precisely because of that lighthouse.

The Church, in some ways, can be thought of as a lighthouse, too.

Down through the centuries for nearly two thousand years—she stands on the shores of time, a beacon inviting all people to eternal life.

Not only is the Church like a lighthouse but her rays of light, the beams by which she can be recognized as light, are called signs. These signs are marks identifying Jesus' Church much in the same fashion that rays identify the presence of the lighthouse. The chief marks of the Church are four: she is one, holy, catholic or universal and apostolic. Only the Catholic Church has these four identifying marks. She is also imperishable or indefectible, which means that the Church will last until the end of time. We will look briefly at the four marks, which are guarantees of the divine seal of the Founder.

G. K. Chesterton

The four marks of the Church

The Catholic Church is *one*. By this is meant that the Church is one in doctrine (truths of Faith and moral code), in worship, and in government. All Catholics are united through their bishops to the Pope.

The Catholic Church is *holy* because her Founder and His doctrine are holy; because her Source of supernatural life, the Holy Spirit, is holy, and because her sacraments give grace which makes people holy.

The Catholic Church is *catholic* or *universal* because it is meant for all people of all places.

The Catholic Church is *apostolic* which means it can be traced back in its foundation to the Apostles, and to St. Peter, the Rock, upon whom the Church was started by Jesus (see: Matthew 16:18).

Converts—those who are not baptized in the Catholic Church as infants but who become Catholics later on—are often attracted to the Catholic Church by a particular one of her marks. The colorful British writer, G. K. Chesterton, as an Anglican, traveled often with his Anglican wife. Their tourist interest and love for religious ceremonies led them now and then into a Catholic Church. After a while, Mr. Chesterton noticed that the Catholics in Rome believed in God and worshiped Him in the same manner that the Catholics in the Holy Land did. The Catholics in the Holy Land believed in God and worshiped Him in the same way that the Catholics in his own native England did. There had to be more than just natural bonds. Such a phenomenon had to be rooted in the divine. The *unity* of the Church led G. K. Chesterton into the fold.

Others are attracted by the Church's saints who were ordinary human beings who became models of holiness. Their stories make fascinating reading. Have you ever read the life of a saint?

Think about it

Each of the marks helps us to love and cherish the Church always more.

The Church, for example, is one. Catholics all over the world, of every race, culture, ethnic background and of every time in history since the Church's beginning, have believed the same truths, worshiped God in the same manner, and have obeyed the same teaching authority—the Pope and bishops. There is a timeless unity.

The Church is holy in her Founder and in her doctrine. She is holy in her sacraments and in her saints. The Church is catholic, meaning universal. All people are part of her great family. All people are invited to share in the Church's spiritual treasures. The Church's apostolicity means that her beginnings can be traced right back to Jesus Himself who founded His Church on the Apostles. The Catholic Church, then, is Jesus' Church. The Church is necessary for salvation, because all the grace that comes from Christ is communicated through His Church. People who do not belong to the Catholic Church can be saved if through no fault of their own they do not know our Savior Jesus Christ or that Christ's Church is truly the Catholic Church, but they do seek God sincerely and try to live good lives with His help.

In the seventeenth century, the faithless philosopher, Voltaire, called the Church "the infamous thing." Three centuries later, a great Pope, Paul VI, in one of his Wednesday general audiences, called the Church "a many-splendored thing." Pope Paul's description offers material for endless reflection because he meditated on and appreciated the great gift that the Church is. It is Jesus' own means of salvation, present in the world until the end of time. The Church ever remains a lighthouse, beckoning all to the port of eternal life. She is called catholic because she is universal and welcomes all to the home of the eternal Father.

Evidence of Jesus in my life

Do I cultivate thoughts of gratitude for the great gift of my Catholic Faith? Do I pray often for those who have fallen away from the Church or who do not know her?

Prayer

Lord, while I think of the Church as a lighthouse
making the way clear to the port of eternal life,
I can't help but face the reality that I, too,
have something to do with people's image
of the Catholic Church.
Teach me to correct in myself all that which is
not worthy of a follower of Yours.
Make me a genuine reflector of Your light.
Help me to take my Faith more seriously and to
love my Church more deeply.
Help me to be an apostle by the way I live my life.

His Mother and Ours

Her story begins in the mind of God when He planned, in His mercy, to redeem us. To the tempting serpent in the Garden of Eden, God said:

...“I will put enmity between you and the woman,
and between your seed and her seed;
He shall bruise your head,
and you shall bruise his heel.”

(Genesis 3:15)

The woman of whom the Lord was speaking was Mary, the Mother of His Son.

Centuries passed. The Chosen People kept the cherished hope of a Messiah alive. Every Jewish family dreamed that their daughter would be the Mother of the Savior. For Joachim and Anne, the dream came true. Their daughter, Mary, a teenager, might have been praying or reading the Scriptures when the Archangel Gabriel appeared to announce, “Do not fear, Mary. You have found favor with God. You shall conceive and bear a son and give him the name Jesus” (Luke 1:30-31). By the Annunciation is meant the day on which the Church recalls the Angel Gabriel’s announcement to Mary, her acceptance, and the Incarnation of Jesus, the Son of God. The feast is celebrated on March 25.

Reflecting on the stupendous reality of Jesus in Mary's womb, we can appreciate what that reality implies. First of all, because Jesus, who is God, was to become physically present in Mary, *she was preserved from original sin from the moment of her conception* in the womb of her mother, St. Anne. This great privilege was granted to Mary in view of the merits of her divine Son. It was proclaimed a dogma of faith by Pope Pius IX in 1854 and is called the Immaculate Conception.

The Son of God became a man at the moment in which Mary agreed to become His mother. The second Person of the Blessed Trinity took a human body and soul in her womb, through the power of the Holy Spirit. Jesus' only Father is God the Father. Jesus' foster father and His guardian was good St. Joseph. Mary is the only woman who is both virgin and mother. Mary's giving birth to Jesus is called the virgin-birth. By the virgin-birth is meant that our Lady remained a virgin before, during and after the birth of Jesus, her only Child.

Think about it

Mary was singularly loved by God and was chosen to be the Mother of His only Son. We might be awed by His choice and wonder how He selected Mary. It is one of the secrets of His love. We admire our Lady's great privileges: her Immaculate Conception, the Annunciation, the virgin-birth, and her Assumption (the special privilege by which Mary's body, freed from corruption, was taken into heaven). It is only right to admire these privileges. But Mary can also be imitated for the heroic manner in which she lived her earthly life.

We can imitate the Mother of God who said: "I am the servant of the Lord. Let it be done to me as you say" (Luke 1:38). Mary is the model and example of faithfully doing the will of God.

Treasured glimpses

The Angel Gabriel's greeting (see: Luke 1:26ff.), and the praise of her cousin, Elizabeth: "Blessed are you among women and blessed is the fruit of your womb" (Luke 1:42), must have made Mary marvel at the goodness of God because she recognized that she was merely His creature. It was genuine humility that led Mary to exclaim:

"For he who is mighty has done
great things for me,
and holy is his name" (Luke 1:49).

Mary's thoughtful regard for her older cousin, St. Elizabeth, caused Mary to go and visit her. She remained several months in her cousin's home caring for her, since Elizabeth was expecting a child. Elizabeth's son, still in her womb, was John the Baptizer.

Mary's faith was valiant as she gave birth to her Son in a stable in Bethlehem. With St. Joseph at her side, she laid her Baby in an animal manger, gazed into His face and adored Him, her God. The Holy Family was ignored by the town of Bethlehem which was filled to overflowing with travelers due to the census of Caesar Augustus. But the Savior of the world was welcomed all the same by angels and poor shepherds (see: Luke 2:14ff.).

Twelve years later Mary and Joseph had to go and search the busy streets of Jerusalem for Jesus. The Holy Family had gone to Jerusalem and Jesus had remained behind. After three days of worry, they found Him. He was in the temple, sitting with the learned teachers. "'How is it you sought for me?' Jesus asked. 'Did you not know that I must be in my Father's house?' And they did not understand the saying which he spoke to them" (Luke 2:49-50). Mary knew that her Child had a special mission, a special work to fulfill. She would learn to trust, to wait, to have patience. Always with her were the haunting words of the holy old prophet, Simeon, spoken when Joseph and Mary had presented the infant Jesus in the Temple. Simeon had blessed the Holy Family and then in hushed earnest, had said to Jesus' Mother:

"Behold, this child is set for the fall and rising of many in Israel...and a sword will pierce through your own soul also" (Luke 2:34-35).

Mary, God's privileged one, was to become for us a model of faithfulness amid the inevitable trials that cross the path of every human being. Mary's sinlessness did not exempt her from suffering, because suffering is not necessarily the result of personal sin. The shadow of Simeon's prophecy loomed over her even in the joyful times, when she slipped into the crowds and listened to the magnetic words of her Son, the Divine Teacher. How the people loved Him! How intently they listened to Him! She watched Him perform miracles. In fact, Mary herself asked for a miracle at Cana of Galilee (see: John 2:1-11). What moments of joy must have been hers when she witnessed her Child fulfilling His ministry.

But the days, weeks and months of Jesus' public life passed. Then came Judas' betrayal, the trials, the final condemnation by Pontius Pilate and the shameful death by crucifixion. Here Jesus' holy Mother Mary emerged from the anonymous crowds to stand in clear relief beneath the cross. She was there to console and to claim her Son. Simeon's prophecy seemed to tear right through her as surely as the sword he had predicted. But Mary believed that the crucifixion was not an end. And she was right. From crucifixion and death came our redemption. After death came Easter Sunday.

Think about it

While He hung in agony, shortly before His death, Jesus looked down at the Apostle John and then at His Mother and said: "'Woman, behold your son.' In turn he said to the disciple, 'Behold your mother'" (John 19:26-27). In this loving gesture, Jesus gave His followers into the care of the human being most dear to Him, His own Mother. From that day on, we, with St. John, the beloved Apostle, would be her children.

Mary was present at the Ascension, and with the company of Apostles and disciples she awaited the coming of the Holy Spirit (see: Acts 1:14). The last New Testament glimpse we have of her is there in the midst of the Apostles, joining them in prayer, encouraging them with her example of fortitude and serenity. She, Jesus' own Mother, is Queen of the Apostles. She is the model of any and every apostle who strives to follow her Son. St. Grignon de Montfort used to say: "To Jesus through Mary."

On the coat of arms, the symbol of his pontificate, Pope John Paul II has a large "M" for Mary with the Latin words, *Totus tuus,* meaning: "All yours."

Catholics show their love for the Mother of God in various ways: by wearing her *scapular,* by placing statues or pictures of Mary in their home so as to be reminded of her. Catholics also honor Mary by making the *Five First Saturdays* and by reciting the *rosary* often, even every day.

Jesus, the Son of God, came to this earth through Mary, His Mother. What better way for us to go to Jesus than through Jesus' Mother. Saints in every age of the Church's history have loved, honored and depended on Mary. Devotion to Mary is the easiest and fastest way to become a saint because by praying to Jesus through Mary we shall receive graces far beyond our due. We shall receive them in proportion to Mary's holiness and not according to our own unworthiness since we will have joined our prayers to hers. With this outpouring of abundant grace our weak human nature so prone to resist the grace of God will be so much more disposed to cooperate with Jesus as He exerts His divine influence over our minds, hearts and wills.

Mary can be compared to a catalyst that causes a chemical reaction or to a bridge uniting an island to the mainland. Our devotion to Mary, who reflects Jesus perfectly, will be the determining factor as to whether or not we reach the goal Jesus has set for us:

"You, therefore, must be perfect as your heavenly Father is perfect."

(Matthew 5:48)

Evidence of Jesus in my life

Just as the Lord was greatly devoted to His Mother Mary, so I must be convinced of my need for her powerful guidance. How often do I think of Mary as my heavenly Mother, and pray to her?

Prayer

Remember, O most gracious Virgin Mary, that never was it known that anyone who fled to your protection, implored your assistance or sought your intercession was left unaided. Inspired with this confidence, we fly to you, O Virgin of virgins, our Mother; to you we come, before you we kneel, sinful and sorrowful. O Mother of the Word Incarnate, despise not our petitions, but in your clemency hear and answer them. Amen.

St. Bernard

His Saving Actions

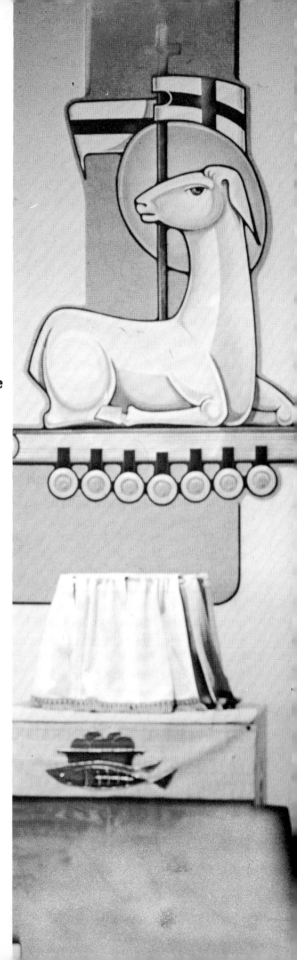

- Baptism, one of the seven sacraments instituted by Jesus, initiates us into Jesus' life of grace.

- The Eucharist is a sacrament, a sacrifice, and the abiding presence of Jesus Himself.

- In Confirmation, we are sealed and strengthened as Christ's witnesses.

- Holy Orders is the ordination of deacons, priests and bishops.

- In the sacrament of Reconciliation, our sins are forgiven by the priest who acts in Jesus' name.

- Matrimony is the sacrament of Christian marriage.

- The Anointing of the Sick consoles the ill and elderly.

Divine Gift

Because we take the study of our Catholic Faith seriously, we see horizons opening up before us—spiritual horizons that we might never have thought of before. The Divine Teacher went back to heaven two thousand years ago, but He left us every gift to provide for our spiritual growth. The gifts are dispensed through His Church. Although we may not have thought about it much before, God wants us to be holy. Holy means "like God" or "close to God." Now, how can we realistically be holy? On our own, we can't. By our own human strength, we can't. But with God's grace, we can.

Through the sacraments, Jesus makes His people holy by means of His grace. (Grace is His life in us, His friendship with us, His presence in us.) Through some of the sacraments Jesus also forgives sins, and through all of them He gives help to avoid sin.

The sacraments are sacred signs through which Jesus gives us His Spirit and makes us holy and pleasing to Him by grace. Every sacrament is a particular gift from Jesus, through His Holy Spirit, to the individual soul. Jesus always gives grace through the sacraments if we receive them under the proper conditions. How greatly the sacrament and its grace will affect us depends on our own attitude, for example, how much faith and love we have.

Think about it

Sometimes we think we need all kinds of things that make our physical living easier. Do we ever find ourselves spending a good deal of time worrying about the acquiring of something that, in all honesty, we could live without? How much time, on the other hand, do we spend thinking about caring for our souls? For example, by:

— participating every Sunday in the Eucharistic Liturgy and receiving Holy Communion with love and attention

— receiving the sacrament of Reconciliation regularly (about twice a month)

— saying morning and evening prayers

— talking to God often throughout the day.

Our spiritual needs and obligations are extremely important and should fill our thoughts, too. If we want to be more faithful to our life as Catholics, we need supernatural strength that comes from grace. Grace comes to us richly through the sacraments, which are Jesus' own saving actions in each of our lives.

Starting out

The seven sacraments are:
- Baptism
- Confirmation
- Holy Eucharist
- Penance
- Anointing of the Sick
- Holy Orders
- Matrimony

Divine Revelation tells us that Jesus instituted all seven sacraments. We may also speak of the Church as a "sacrament"—a great sacrament through which we receive the other seven. The Church is a sign that there is a God, and that He cares about the world. The sacraments, too, are signs of God's loving concern for people.

Our sacramental life begins with Baptism. Most of us received this sacrament while we were still babies. The priest poured water on our forehead and said: "I baptize you in the name of the Father, and of the Son, and of the Holy Spirit." The simultaneous pouring of water and saying the words produce singular effects:

—Jesus sends us His Spirit, who frees us from sin, original sin and personal sin, if any;

—Jesus gives us the grace by which we become God's children, heirs of heaven, members of the Church and temples of the Blessed Trinity. When we have grace in our souls, we can truly say that God lives in us in a particular way;

—Jesus gives us a spiritual banquet: sanctifying grace, the theological or God-given virtues, and the seven gifts of the Holy Spirit.

In Baptism we also receive a *lasting spiritual seal* called a character, which sets us apart as belonging to Jesus Christ. Any unbaptized person may receive Baptism which is so necessary because it takes away original sin and gives us the life of grace. Because of that lasting spiritual seal, we cannot be baptized more than once.

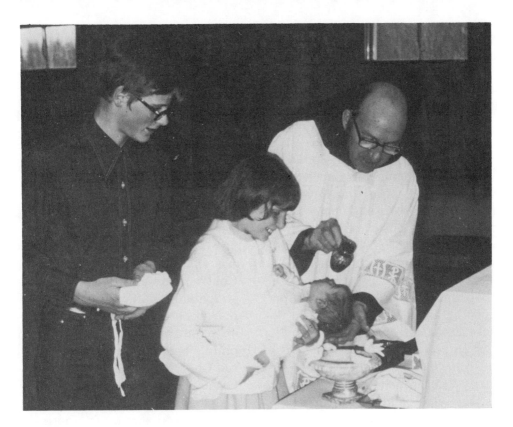

Baptism is a vital sacrament. It initiates us into the life of grace. The Church baptizes infants for just this reason and obliges Catholic parents to have their babies baptized within the first few weeks after birth. While an infant should not be baptized without the permission of a parent or guardian, except when in danger of death, we should encourage Catholic parents, or a single Catholic parent, whenever possible, to have the child baptized soon. Catholic parents who put off for a long time, or entirely neglect, the Baptism of their children may put them in the danger of losing the vision of God eternally.

Great numbers of infants, especially because of the rampant crime of abortion, die unbaptized. But they have committed no sins. It has been generally held by many in the Church that these babies will live in a place of natural happiness. We know that God's infinite love will provide for each of His children.

If an unbaptized person has reached what is called the *age of reason* that is, able to understand, he or she must first receive religious instuction before being baptized. He or she must also have faith and sorrow for sin with the intention of avoiding future sin.

The ordinary minister of Baptism is the bishop, priest or deacon, but in the danger of death, anyone may and sometimes should baptize. In secular hospitals that perform abortions, Catholic nurses frequently succeed in baptizing children aborted alive.

In an emergency, the person who baptizes can be anyone: man, woman or child, Catholic or non-Catholic, atheist or pagan, as long as he or she administers the sacrament properly and does it with the intention of "doing what the Church does."

Emergency Baptism is given by pouring ordinary water on the forehead of the person to be baptized, saying while pouring it: "I baptize you in the name of the Father, and of the Son, and of the Holy Spirit." The words must be said at the same time the water is poured.

This great sacrament is necessary for salvation, yet those who through no fault of their own have not received or have not even heard about Baptism, can be saved through what is called Baptism of Blood or Baptism of Desire.

Baptism of Blood is the reception of grace by an unbaptized person because he or she gives his or her life for love of Christ or a Christian virtue. We know of examples from the early Church that when Christians were being killed, their heroic example at times influenced the Roman soldiers, who though unbaptized, would also declare their belief in Jesus at the cost of their lives. The martyred soldiers received Baptism of Blood.

Baptism of Desire is the reception of grace because of perfect love of God or perfect sorrow for sin and the desire to do His will. In other words, if a person had known of Baptism and was able to receive it, he would be baptized.

Everyone who receives Baptism has at least one godparent (or sponsor)—a responsible Catholic who has already received Baptism, Confirmation and Eucharist. A godparent testifies to the faith of the one to be baptized, or in the case of an infant he or she, together with the child's parents, professes the Faith of the Church. Occasionally, a non-Catholic Christian can act as a Christian witness along with one Catholic godparent. (The norms for various ecumenical cases should be followed. The parish priest would know what these are.)

Think about it

Most of us were baptized as babies. Baptism marked a great day in our lives. Through our godparents, we made sacred promises to renounce the devil, his allurements, or temptations, and to live according to the teachings of Christ and His Church. We were also given a name.

A saint's name is given in Baptism so that the new Christian will have a protector in heaven to imitate and ask for help. That patron becomes our patron saint.

We have a lot to think about.... Promises to God must be kept. Promises to God can be kept if we ask God for the grace to be faithful unto death. Ask Him, too, to help us grow in appreciation for Baptism which is a gift to us, and to remember always that non-Catholics will often be attracted to the Church by the way we live our baptismal commitment.

Evidence of Jesus in my life

I cannot just pick and choose my own norms of morality or the way in which I will worship God. I have the voice of the Church directing me. And that voice is for me the will of God.

Prayer

Jesus, Divine Teacher,
You sent Your Apostles to
baptize all nations.

Today, Your missionaries all over
the world never cease bringing Your
message to everyone.

Help me, by my reflection on
this sacrament of Baptism, to deepen
my love for Jesus and His Church.

Help me to be an apostle, too, in
my own little way, grateful for what I
have been given,

and in my enthusiasm, spreading
the Faith to others.

Never let me forget Your words
to the Apostles:

"The gift you have received, give
as a gift" (Matthew 10:8).

The Presence

The priest looked at his small congregation gathered at morning weekday Mass. The devout people followed the Mass with fervor. The moment of consecration arrived. The priest's hands trembled slightly as he picked up the host and began to enunciate slowly and clearly: "This is my body...." But his mind was racing. "I can't go on like this," the priest said to himself. "I'm a hypocrite. I don't believe. I just can't believe." By the end of the Mass, he had reached a decision. Admitting his doubts about the Real Presence of Christ in the Eucharist, he would make a trip to Rome on foot and by donkey to see the Pope. The prospect of making such a journey from his distant land to Rome in the eleventh century meant danger and privation. But no price was too much if once again he could find peace of mind.

The troubled priest began his journey. Each evening, he found refuge in a rectory along the way and in the morning would celebrate Mass before continuing his sorrowful journey. What would he say to the Pope? How would he begin? What would the Pope say? What would the Pope do? As night approached, he neared a little town called Bolsena in Italy. The next morning he celebrated Mass in the small parish church. A few people were present. The priest mechanically fulfilled each part of the Mass. As he began the "Lamb of God," perspiration formed on his forehead and in the palm of his hands. The old doubts surged through him. The priest carefully broke the host in two and said: "Behold, the Lamb of God...." His hands seemed to freeze on the host. He stared in wonder as blood began

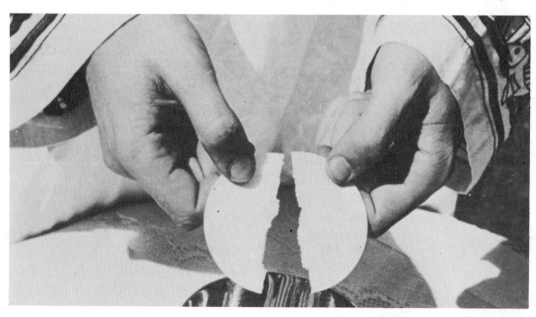

to ooze from the torn host. He hastily tried to put the consecrated bread back together but in vain. Blood spilled onto the corporal, then on the altar cloth. The priest knelt down, eyes glued to the bleeding host, and repeated the words Thomas the Apostle had exclaimed centuries before: "My Lord and my God." Gone were the doubts. Gone were the torments and fears. Peace flooded the priest's soul.

The town's people clustered around the wondrous sight and adored the bleeding host. Story of the miracle spread and the bloodstained corporal was carefully preserved and remains intact to this day in the beautiful basilica erected in nearby Orvietto to commemorate the miracle.

The Eucharist—a miracle

In the Old Testament, God sent manna—a wafer-like bread—to feed the Chosen People as they wandered during their forty years in the desert. In the New Testament, Jesus talks about bread...the bread of life (see: John 6). At the Last Supper, with His Apostles, the night before He died, Jesus instituted the Holy Eucharist:

"Now as they were eating, Jesus took bread, and blessed, and broke it, and gave it to the disciples and said, 'Take, eat; this is my body.' And he took a cup, and when he had given thanks he gave it to them, saying, 'Drink of it, all of you; for this is my blood of the covenant, which is poured out for many for the forgiveness of sins.'"

(Matthew 26:26-28)

The Apostles were present at the Last Supper, the first Eucharistic Celebration. Jesus gave us the Holy Eucharist because He wants to stay close to His followers until the end of time to teach us, comfort us, strengthen us and make us holy.

The Holy Eucharist is a sacrament, a sacrifice and the abiding presence of Jesus Himself, God and man. He is truly and completely present under the appearances of bread and wine. He makes us more like Himself and joins us to one another. The Eucharist is different from all the other sacraments because under the appearances of bread and wine *Jesus is completely present as both God and man.* In the other sacraments, He is present only by His power and its effects.

Think about it

The Eucharist is bread consecrated by the priest who acts in the person of Jesus. The priest, at every Eucharistic Celebration or Mass, repeats the words that Jesus spoke: "This is my body; this is my blood." Bread and wine are instantly and totally changed into the Body and Blood of Christ. The bread still looks like bread, but it is not bread. It has become the Body of Christ. The wine still looks and smells like wine, but it is not wine. It has become the Blood of Christ. The Eucharist, then, is Jesus Himself in our midst. The Eucharist becomes present at the Mass or Eucharistic Celebration. This miraculous change of bread and wine into the Body and Blood of Christ is called *Transubstantiation.*

119

The Mass and Jesus' death on Calvary

The words of consecration—"This is my body which will be given up for you..."; "This is the cup of my blood.... It will be shed for you"...—tell us that the Eucharist is the Body and Blood of Jesus, and that Christ is offered in sacrifice. But, we might ask, how does the Mass relate to Jesus' death on the cross? In other words, how is the Mass a sacrifice?

If you should sit down to a table of bread and wine, it would not convey the notion of death to you, would it? But let us examine the reality before us at Mass. Picture Jesus in your mind hanging on the cross at Calvary. St. John tells us that when the soldier pierced His side with a lance, blood and water flowed out.

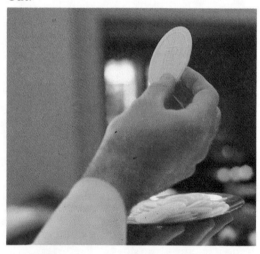

So Jesus' Body was now on the cross; but His Blood had been shed. His Blood was separated from His Body. At the consecration, the priest changes the bread into the Body of Christ. Then he reverently lays It on the altar.

Next, he changes the wine into the precious Blood of Jesus. Then (after the elevation) he also lays It reverently next to Christ's Body (the host). So with your own eyes at Mass, you see Jesus' true Body and Blood separated. This "shows forth" His death, it is not a physical death. It is a death sign. St. Paul assures us that "Christ having died once, dies now no more: death shall no longer have dominion over him." It is, instead, Christ's death on Calvary in sacramental form.

Another way of saying this is: it is a "mystical death." The words of consecration are like a sword, mystically (but not factually) separating the Body (host) from the Blood (wine) of Christ.

One final point: if we receive only the sacred host in Communion, we are also receiving the Blood of Christ. We are receiving the Body and Blood of Christ. This is because Jesus is totally present in His sacred Body and in His sacred Blood.

On Calvary, Christ was present as He then was. In the Mass, Christ is present as He now is. And He is now in heaven in His risen Body, living and glorious. His sacred wounds plead for us constantly before the face of His Father, our Father. Once so painful, so torturing: His wounds are now trophies of victory, tokens of deepest love for each one of us.

Think about it

The importance of the Eucharist can never be over-stressed because the Eucharist is Jesus Himself. The main purposes of the Mass are:
— to adore (praise) God
— to thank Him
— to ask His forgiveness
— to atone (make up) for sin
— to ask His help for ourselves and others.

The Mass is so powerful because in it Jesus Himself prays to the Father for us. Because of the importance of the Mass, the Church obliges us to go to Mass on Sundays and holy days of obligation. The late Cardinal Cushing of Boston used to call Mass: "the biggest daily event in your neighborhood." If you know some Catholics who do not participate in Sunday Mass, then we realize it can only be because they have never learned or have forgotten the treasure that the Mass is.

A share in infinite riches

Participating in the Mass with attention and love can help us:
— to avoid temptations and sin
— to find peace of mind and heart
— to grow in the love of God
— to obtain protection against all dangers
— to gain the help we need from God
— to shorten the purgatory of departed family members and friends.

We are also invited to receive Jesus in Holy Communion provided we are ready. We must: believe that the Eucharist is Jesus, be free from mortal sin, and have fasted for at least one hour from food and drink (except water or medicine). The elderly and those who are suffering from illness, as well as those who care for them (including visitors and family members who provide moral and emotional support), may receive the Blessed Eucharist even if within the preceding hour they have consumed something.

Catholics who have made their first Communion are to take part in the Mass every Sunday (or Saturday night) and receive Communion at least once a year (usually between the first Sunday in Lent and Trinity Sunday. For a good reason the precept may be fulfilled at another time during the year). This obligation is called our "Easter Duty." Receiving Communion once a year, of course, is only the minimum. We should receive Jesus in Holy Communion often, even every day, because it is Jesus who makes us holy by giving us His life and grace.

Think about it

Jesus, our Savior, has given us every supernatural help for reaching heaven. The Eucharist is the great treasure of "Himself." The Eucharist is the Mass; the Eucharist is our food in Holy Communion; the Eucharist is the Real Presence of Jesus remaining in the Tabernacles of every Catholic Church. The more we become aware of the Church's spiritual treasures, the more we appreciate and love the Holy Eucharist. We love the Sunday and weekday celebration of Mass. We love the Liturgical Year. This is the name given to the days and seasons within a year's time in which the Church celebrates Christ's Paschal Mystery. The liturgical seasons are Advent, Christmas, Lent, Easter and Ordinary Time. Sundays and holy days, feasts of Mary, celebrations of saints' days and other feast days light the Church year with warmth to stir the devotion of God's people.

Jesus' abiding presence in the Tabernacle

Have you ever lingered after Mass and seen the number of people who remain motionless in their pew or who have moved to the front of the Church kneeling before the Tabernacle? Our Faith teaches us that Jesus remains totally present in the host after Mass to be adored by the faithful. What reason did Jesus intend with His abiding presence? All the saints would agree with St. Thomas Aquinas who admitted that whatever he learned from studying books of theology seemed next to nothing compared to the inspirations he received on his knees before Jesus in the Blessed Sacrament.

Evidence of Jesus in my life

Do I realize that receiving the sacred host means receiving Jesus Himself? Do I prepare seriously for Communion, making sure that I am free from serious sin and have kept the necessary fast? Do I remain in silent thankfulness for an appropriate time after receiving Holy Communion?

Prayer

Jesus, Divine Teacher, once You told the crowds:
"I am the living bread
which came down from heaven;
if anyone eats of this bread,
he will live for ever;
and the bread which I will give
for the life of the world is my flesh" (John 6:51).

Many who listened to You that day walked away
and never came back.
I don't want to make the same sad mistake.
Instead, I believe that You are the living bread
of the Eucharist.
I want to receive You very often.
Help me to be ready to receive You often.
You are the Bread of Life (see: John 6:35).
You are the "way, and the truth and the life"
(John 14:6).

Be Your Best, Give the Best

The word "witness" is frequently heard today. For example, a person can be a witness in court or we can witness an event. Whether used as a noun (witness in court), or a verb (to witness an event), the word has a particular meaning when we study about the powerful gift of the sacrament of Confirmation. Some people might think of Confirmation as a kind of "graduation" from the study and practice of their Catholic Faith, but we will see that there is no such thing as graduating from the study and practice of our religion.

The Holy Spirit came into our souls for the first time when we received the sacrament of Baptism, most likely as infants. He remains with us to help us grow in grace day by day. However, with the sacrament of Confirmation, the Holy Spirit increases His presence and the effects of His presence in a unique way. In the sacrament, a Christian receives a second, spiritual seal which lasts forever. The first lasting spiritual seal was received at Baptism. This seal is called a character. Confirmed Catholics become full-fledged members of the Church. They receive spiritual strength and more actual graces to help them to better witness to Christ. The confirmed have also grown in the graces and gifts first received in Baptism. This is indicated during the Confirmation ceremony when the Holy Spirit is called upon to come with His seven gifts.

Think about it

Confirmation is the sacrament in which the Holy Spirit comes to us in a special way to join us more closely to Jesus and His Church and to seal and strengthen us as Christ's witnesses. To confirm means to strengthen. With this sacrament, the Holy Spirit works actively in us. He deepens and strengthens our faith. He helps us to realize that through Confirmation we are more perfectly bound to Christ and His Church.

What each of us has to do is allow the grace of Confirmation to work in us. Every human being has a free will. We can use our will to grow closer to God and be generous witnesses of Christ, or we can let ourselves be side-tracked by our selfish wants and narrow goals. Confirmation is not just a ritual, or a beautiful celebration to enjoy for the moment and then forget. Confirmation is an obligation and an opportunity. It is a personal commitment for each one of us to become the best Catholic ever.

What is expected of us

Any baptized Catholic, who has not been confirmed, may receive Confirmation. The Church urges Catholics to study their Faith well before receiving Confirmation because a confirmed Catholic is expected to live up to his or her Faith. What does it mean "to live up to one's Faith"? This means that the Church teaches divinely revealed truths that come from her Founder, Jesus. We must be taught those truths in order to believe and love them. The Church teaches the Gospel morality taught and lived by Jesus. We must be imbued with that morality, too, in order to mold our lives on Christian values and make correct moral choices. Living up to our Faith calls for a deepening awareness of the importance of God's grace in us. We deepen our belief in the sacraments and receive Holy Communion and Penance often.

What if until now we have not put forth enough effort in the study and practice of our Faith? It is easy enough to set our priorities right. All we need is will power and prayer. Preparing for Confirmation takes genuine internal discipline. A Catholic should prepare for Confirmation by studying the Catholic Faith, by praying, and as mentioned earlier in this lesson, by witnessing to Christ.

Witnessing to Christ is both simple and complicated. It is simple, meaning "not complex." Witnessing, first of all, involves the giving of good example. What we say and what we do are our first priorities in preparing for Confirmation. We have to ask ourselves honestly:

Are the words I say words that Jesus could and would say?

Are my actions what Jesus would do? Do I perform my actions the way Jesus would?

When it comes to words and actions, we can't stop there, either. We have to ask another question: Did I go out of my way to say a good word or do a possible good deed even when it was "beyond duty"? This is to be a witness to Christ. A witness to Christ is a person who tells or shows others something about Christ. We witness to Christ by learning, living, loving, standing up for and sharing our Catholic Faith. The learning, living, loving, standing up for and sharing our Catholic Faith is not something we do once or twice and then lay aside. Our Catholic Faith means everything that we believe and do as Catholics. It is a *permanent commitment* that calls for will power and prayer. The sacrament of Confirmation should make us realize that there is no such

thing as a part-time Catholic or a Sunday Catholic.

Sometimes we try to create a soft, patterned, comfortable life for ourselves. We envy those who seem to have every earthly comfort and might aspire to such a goal ourselves. In fact, we could even make our highest goal financial success. But the person who takes his or her Catholic Faith seriously cannot be locked into such narrow goals that lead to selfishness. The sacrament of Confirmation calls us to unselfishness, and not only that, to heroic dedication.

Think about it

If we love God, we also love our neighbor. We begin doing what we can to make a better world. Father James Keller, founder of the Christophers, used to say: "It is better to light one candle than to curse the darkness!"

The bishop is the ordinary minister of Confirmation. In the Church's name, the bishop sends confirmed Christians out on a mission—to spread the Faith by word and example. We spread Christ's Faith among our own family and relatives, in our neighborhood, at school, among friends and acquaintances. That is the way to light our one candle. The sacrament of Confirmation consists of anointing and words. The bishop extends his hands over the person and anoints the forehead in the form of a cross while saying: "Be sealed with the Gift of the Holy Spirit." The person being confirmed answers, "Amen," meaning, "Let it be so." Our "Amen" means that we want to light our candle, and we ask the Holy Spirit to keep it shining bright.

Evidence of Jesus in my life

Am I willing to honestly admit my attitude about receiving Confirmation? Is it because I want to become a more fervent Catholic, more generous and self-sacrificing? This should be my only attitude. I want to ask Jesus to help me prepare for this great event in my life by much prayer and serious study.

Prayer

Jesus, Divine Teacher,
help me to appreciate the sacrament of Confirmation.
Let me realize that when the bishop anoints me on the forehead,
in the form of a cross, I am showing You that I am
proud of my Faith, and, with Your help,
will witness to it even in the
face of difficulties.
Keep close to me, Lord, and remind me often
of the Holy Spirit's presence in my soul.
Help me never to take my Catholic Faith for granted.

You Are a Priest Forever...

We have already studied about the wonder of the Eucharist, the sacrament of Jesus' own Body and Blood, and have thought deeply about the great treasure that it is. The Eucharist, nourishment of God's people, comes to us, as we know, through the Eucharistic Celebration. This realization leads us, then, to another great sacrament that gives us priests: the sacrament of Holy Orders. So tied together are the sacraments of Eucharist and Holy Orders that it can be truthfully concluded that without Holy Orders there can be no Eucharist. In many parts of the world, Catholic communities wait for priests to come among them to celebrate the Eucharist and forgive their sins in the sacrament of Reconciliation.

Pope John Paul II, in one of his homilies, told of the small, fervent group of Catholics in a town where no priest was available for miles. Every Sunday, the people gathered for the Liturgy of the Word—a service of sacred readings and prayers. A set of priest's vestments, the alb and the stole were placed reverently on the altar, symbolic of their hope that a priest would soon come to stay permanently among them.

What is so special about Holy Orders or the priesthood? Holy Orders is the sacrament through which men are given the grace and power to carry out the sacred duties of deacons, priests or bishops. The priesthood is a calling or vocation from God. He invites those whom He chooses to follow Him more closely,

to be consecrated to Him in a particular way. The only explanation for His calling and choice is love. God is infinite. He also loves infinitely. He loves each human being infinitely, but in different ways and degrees. We are challenged to love Him in return and to live according to His will in our life.

The call to priesthood is a singular gift. Priests have the God-given power to imitate Jesus in a special way by celebrating Mass and changing bread and wine into Jesus' Body and Blood. They also forgive sins in Jesus' name and bring His comfort in the Anointing of the Sick. Besides this, priests can do everything that deacons can do. And

in certain cases, priests can also administer Confirmation.

The priesthood is a special privilege. No one has a *right* to be ordained. A man is called to the priesthood by God through His Church. Therefore, ordination is God's gift to him, not his right.

Think about it

Priests of the *Latin rite* are consecrated to celibacy, to remain unmarried. We might like to think of this consecration in view of what priests receive—the priceless gift of Holy Orders. Holy Orders is a supernatural gift, above the natural. Nothing in the natural order that a priest has to give up could ever compare with the joys he receives from his great vocation. He acts for Jesus in the Mass and various sacraments. He deserves and receives the love and respect of the people whom he spiritually cares for in the name of Jesus. He is listened to and obeyed in all his teaching that truly reflects Christ and His Church. And because he, like us, is a human being

with a wounded human nature, we pray and make sacrifices for him.

St. Theresa of Lisieux, who died in her early twenties of tuberculosis, never left her cloistered Carmelite monastery. Yet, she has been proclaimed patron saint of the missions. How can this be? She never once went out to preach or teach catechism directly, but she prayed for priests all over the world. She made acts of self-denial so that priest-missionaries would have the stamina to continue laboring for Christ. Even though tormented with illness, she offered up every pain for a weary priest, or a faltering priest— whatever priest who somewhere in the world needed that sacrifice.

The merciful Savior accepted St. Theresa's prayers and sacrifices. Many a priest in a faraway land benefited by the generosity of the young cloistered sister whom they did not know and who never stepped outside her convent.

The third lasting seal

The bishop acts for Jesus conferring Holy Orders. A man who is a good Catholic, has prepared. himself by study, and has been accepted by the bishop may receive Holy Orders. Holy Orders is given through the bishop's laying on of hands and his prayer that God may give the dignity of the priesthood to the man (or men) being ordained. When this takes place, the man receives more grace, the powers of the priesthood, and a third lasting spiritual seal—the character of a priest. Once ordained, a priest is a priest for all eternity. He is marked or sealed for the Divine Priest, Jesus Christ. Imagine the gratitude to God that a priest should always have.

The sign of Holy Orders is made up of the laying on of hands and a special prayer. The bishop places his hands, palms downward, on the candidate's head to show the giving of the Holy Spirit, with His grace and power.

Priests perform many ministries of service for God's people. Parish priests, also called secular or diocesan, take care of the needs of the people in their parish. They teach the people what the Church teaches, guide their flock in right living and bring them God's grace through the Mass and sacraments. Priests who belong to religious congregations perform the particular mission to which their congregation is dedicated. Many priests in the Church's long history have been declared saints: parish priests like St. John Vianney of Ars, France, and founders of religious communities such as St. Ignatius of Loyola who started the Jesuit Order and St. John Bosco who started the Salesian Order.

Some priests become missionaries—taking the Gospel message to other nations and continents. Others, by their dedication and selfless giving are apostles right in their own parish. Some priests are in the Armed Forces and serve God's people as military chaplains. How important it is to thank God often for sending His priests to bring God's life of grace to us through the sacraments.

Deacons serve the people by baptizing, reading God's Word to the faithful, preaching, distributing Communion, giving Eucharistic Benediction, blessing couples who receive the sacrament of Matrimony, and performing many works of service. There are two kinds of deacons. Men preparing for the priesthood are ordained as deacons before being ordained as priests. They remain deacons only for a time. There are also permanent deacons. These are single and married men who will remain deacons for the rest of their lives.

Think about it

The Divine Teacher walked along the shores of Galilee nearly two thousand years ago and called the Apostles to follow Him (see: Matthew 10:1-4; Mark 3:14-19; Luke 6:12-16).

He calls His special collaborators today as well. The shores of Galilee now extend to the whole world and Jesus calls by speaking to the hearts of individuals of His choice. Priests are God's choice and God's blessings to us. If a young man hears such an invitation, what should he do? First of all, pray with trust to know the Lord's will. He should also receive the sacraments of Eucharist and Penance more frequently and seek spiritual direction from a holy priest.

Evidence of Jesus in my life

Do I realize that without the priesthood, the People of God would have no Eucharist or sacrament of Reconciliation? Every day I will ask Jesus to call many good young men to be priests.

Prayer

Lord Jesus, who called the ones You wanted to call,
call many of us to work for You,
to work with You.
You who enlightened with Your words
those whom You called,
enlighten us with faith in You.
You who supported them in their difficulties,
help us to overcome the difficulties
we have as young people today.
And if You call one of us
to be consecrated completely to You,
may Your love give warmth to this vocation
from its very beginning and make it grow
and persevere to the end. Amen.

Pope John Paul II

Divine Healer

Before we can study about one of the sacraments of healing, the sacrament of Penance or Reconciliation, we must realize that each of us has a basic need for forgiveness. Forgiveness implies guilt and sin. Sin is disobedience to God's law. People begin to be able to commit sin when they reach what is called the "age of reason" (usually around seven or earlier). Personal sin, or sin committed by each of us as individuals, is called *actual sin* and can be of two kinds: *mortal* and *venial*. Every sin, of course, is an offense. The offended one is God. Our Creator is offended by His creatures.

The holy priest of Ars, France, St. John Vianney, would spend as much as sixteen hours every day hearing confessions. As he listened to the sad tale of personal offenses, he would often weep and slowly shake his head, saying softly: "Oh, how much the good God is offended." St. John Vianney grew to love the sacrament of Penance more and more as he understood it to be a channel of God's mercy and love.

Sometimes we find it difficult to forgive another individual who perhaps even unintentionally has hurt us. Yet, the offense is from one human being to another. Imagine the goodness of God who will forgive our sins as often as we wish to be forgiven, as often as we seek forgiveness, in the sacrament of mercy. We tell our sins to the priest who acts in Jesus' name, who takes the place of Jesus. We might be afraid to confess our sins, or even may be ashamed and embarrassed. If we think of ourselves alone with Jesus, then fear vanishes. We have the courage to tell what has to be said. All mortal sins (serious sins) have to be told in confession.

A sin is mortal if:

—it regards a serious matter;

—before or while committing it, the person clearly is aware that it is something wrong. The person is aware of the serious wrong if, at the time he foresees the sin will follow, he knows or at least suspects that the action is grievously sinful. That which is seriously sinful, wrong or evil is known to be such from Sacred

Scripture, Tradition, the teachings of the Church and the dictates of right reason;

—the person freely gives full consent to it. A person fully consents to do wrong when he freely chooses to do evil, although he is entirely free not to do it.

Because we are weak at times, and try to choose the easy road, we have to be firm with ourselves and admit our sins. We might try to fool ourselves and say that a particular action is not sinful when we know it is. But this will never lead to inner peace. Our *conscience* cannot be suppressed. Peace comes from admission of guilt when we have done wrong. Admission of our sins in the sacrament of Reconciliation sets our troubled souls at rest. We leave the confessional with Jesus' blessing, given through His priest: "Go in the peace of Christ." We are free to tell our venial sins in confession, at least those venial sins we find ourselves committing so often: impatience, unkind remarks, gossip, carelessness in our daily duties, etc. Each time we receive the sacrament of mercy with good will we grow in God's love and grace.

Mortal sin deprives the sinner of sanctifying grace, the supernatural life of the soul, and makes the soul an enemy of God. Mortal sin takes away the merit of all the person's good actions, deprives it of the right to everlasting happiness in heaven, and makes it deserving of everlasting punishment in hell.

A person who has committed a mortal sin should say a prayer of perfect sorrow with the intention of going to confession soon. This restores sanctifying grace. But this person may not receive Communion until he has gone to confession. The requirements for confessing mortal sins are: a person should say what kind of sins they were and, as far as possible, tell how many times these sins were committed, as well as any circumstances that might change or modify their nature.

A sin is venial when one of the conditions for a mortal sin is missing. For example, the thought, desire, word, action or omission is wrong but not seriously so, or it is seriously wrong but a person does not clearly see this, or does not fully consent to it. Venial sin harms us by making us care less about God and our Catholic Faith. It makes us weaker when faced with serious sin and temptation, and makes us deserving of God's punishments on this earth and in purgatory. We should avoid venial sins because even though they do not destroy the life of grace, they are an offense to God, and they weaken our friendship with Him. They also dispose us to mortal sin and merit for us some temporal punishment either in this life or in the next.

Think about it

Some people try to ignore the reality of sin. They find it repulsive to think of sin in relation to themselves and those around them. Some even deny that sin exists! But to deny the reality of sin is to deny that we as human beings have free will. Yes, we are free, and though we should always choose good and never evil, we know that at times we have failed. Why is sin so much a part of the human story? As we recalled earlier in our text, our nature has been wounded—not depraved but wounded—by original sin. We feel a certain attraction towards what is evil. Chief among these attractions are the seven capital sins: pride, covetousness, lust, anger, gluttony, envy and sloth. We are also too inclined towards sins of omissions—failing to do what we know we should.

The mercy of Jesus

The more we think about the sacrament of Penance, the more we appreciate the great gift it is. This sacrament is not a courtroom session in which we are placed on trial. It is a spiritual "oasis" where we find the Divine Teacher, the Divine Healer. In order to forgive us in Jesus' name, the priest must know what our sins are. That is why we must say them to the priest. The five steps necessary for receiving the sacrament of Penance worthily are:

1) examination of our conscience
2) contrition (sorrow for our sins)
3) resolution (promise to improve)
4) confession of our sins to the priest
5) acceptance of the penance the priest gives.

Any Catholic who has committed sin may receive the sacrament of Penance. The priest who administers the sacrament of Penance, called a confessor, has the power from Jesus to absolve or "release" us from our sins. We tell our sins to the priest because he has to know what our sins are in order to forgive them in

Christ's name. We confess our sins with the intention of not committing them again. No sin is forgiven by God unless there is supernatural sorrow for it (even imperfect sorrow, such as fear of divine punishment) and a firm resolution not to commit it again.

The Church requires that we receive the sacrament of Penance at least once a year if we have serious sins. But the law is the minimum. Good Catholics try to go once a month, bi-weekly or even weekly, if possible. As we mentioned earlier in this lesson, all mortal sins must be confessed, but we may also confess venial sins and faults. In other words, also that which keeps us from drawing closer to God is subject matter for confession. The seal or secret of confession binds the priest never to reveal to anyone the contents of our confession.

Think about it

When we approach the God of mercy in the sacrament of Penance or Reconciliation with sincerity and faith, we have nothing to lose and everything to gain:

—our sins are forgiven;

—our soul is restored to the state of grace (if we have committed mortal sins), or we grow in sanctifying grace (if we committed only venial sins);

—we are set free from all the eternal punishment and at least some of the temporal punishment due to our sins;

—we receive the sacramental grace of the sacrament of Penance, which strengthens us to avoid sin in the future and the sacrament restores the merits of our good works if they have been lost by mortal sin;

—we receive the help to lead better lives;

—we are reconciled with the Church which we have wounded by our sins.

After we have received the sacrament of Reconciliation, we walk out of Church, knowing with the sureness of faith that we have left our sins behind, so to speak. They have been taken from us by Jesus and nailed to His cross. He paid the price for each of our sins. The Divine Teacher tells us: "I will never leave you unless you chase me away with your serious sins...."

Evidence of Jesus in my life

Do I receive Jesus' gift of the sacrament of Penance often and with sorrow? Am I truthful and sincere, trying my best to make a good confession? If I have to improve on this point, I will ask Jesus for the grace.

Prayer

Give us, Lord, light to form in ourselves
a right conscience;
strengthen us to follow it and preserve us from
yielding to sin.
Guard us from the blindness of mind
and hardness of heart
to which impurity leads.
Grant us openness to Your grace in prayer.
You know our difficulties and the dangers
which surround us,
but You assure us that through prayer and the
frequent reception of Your sacraments we will
never lose heart.
Fill us with a spirit of self-control, for in this way
we will reach the reward of heaven.
And finally give us, O Lord, a true devotion
to Your Mother, Mary.
She is the ever pure Virgin, our model and protectress.
Entrusting our purity to her care,
we need not fear. Amen.

Why Marriage Is Sacred

A successful businessman confided in a letter: "June twenty-ninth, the feast of Sts. Peter and Paul, is the wedding anniversary of my parents. I will always treasure that date because of all that my parents mean to me." Those words reflect a person who treasures the home he came from and the parents who were God's instruments in giving him life and growth as a child of God.

Have you ever looked into the eyes of a frightened child? The fright can be caused by a momentary situation, but it can also be a condition more enduring. And if we were asked to propose a cure...a remedy that would remove the fright, would it not be the love and security of the child's family? From love and security flow stability. Since time has been recorded, families have tried to dig their roots into the earth. They have aspired to own land, build a home on that land and to establish permanent relationships. The most permanent of all human bonds can be found in society's basic "cell," the family.

The family began when, in the book of Genesis, God said: "It is not good that the man should be alone; I will make him a helper fit for him" (Genesis 2:18). God created Eve to be Adam's partner. "Therefore a man leaves his father and mother and cleaves to his wife, and they become one flesh" (Genesis 2:24).

Human life is sacred. Marriage is sacred, so sacred, in fact, that it is raised by Jesus to the dignity of a sacrament. Jesus restored marriage to the status of one husband married to one wife, until death (see: Matthew 19:3ff.). Matrimony is the sacrament through which a baptized man and a baptized woman join themselves for life in a lawful marriage and receive God's grace so that they may carry out their responsibilities. So important is their lifetime contract of fidelity that a husband and wife receive sacramental grace which provides the strength to grow closer to Jesus, to each other, and to the children whom God will send them.

Not only did Jesus propose faithfulness until death to one partner, but He proposed a model family to imitate. If we read the Gospel closely, we can see the Holy Family of Nazareth: Jesus, Mary and Joseph.

St. Joseph, Mary's husband and foster-father of the Son of God, is called the man of silence, but his actions preach an eloquent sermon of fidelity and manly strength. We see his virtue in Matthew 1:18-24; 2:13-23; Luke 2:1-21. Those passages mark two major events in the life of Jesus: His birth and His escape into Egypt, safely brought about by His foster-father, St. Joseph, who out-maneuvered an entire army of the wicked King Herod to bring Mary and Jesus safely into a foreign land.

We see Mary who had given birth to her Child in a stable with a manger for His bed. Christmas cards make the scene so charming, so full of awe, yet...what made that stable different from any other? What "immortalized" it? The presence of the Holy Family: the love and attention of a mother, the strength and practical care of the foster-father, and the presence of the Divine Child. We see them coming to the Temple forty days after Jesus' birth (see: Luke 2:22-35). Twelve years later that same couple was in Jerusalem for the Passover celebration which lasted several days. Joseph and Mary lost Jesus. They searched anxiously for three days, giving themselves no rest until they found their boy. What could they have imagined when they saw Him there among the learned Doctors in the Temple talking about spiritual topics? Overcome with the joy of finding Jesus, and strengthened by God's love and the love of each other, they returned home to Nazareth (see: Luke 2:41-52).

Think about it

When Jesus began His public life, good St. Joseph was no longer mentioned in the Gospels, but we still catch awesome glimpses of Mary. She was at the wedding feast of Cana (see: John 2:1-12); she and Jesus' cousins were in the crowds that heard Him preach (see: Mark 3:31-35); Mary stood beneath His cross (see: John 19:25-30), and received her Son's dead body into her arms.

What can we learn from these events recorded about the Holy Family in the Gospels? We can learn how to love truly, how to be self-sacrificing, loyal and generous. Study these Gospel events yourself and you will find many more virtues apparent in the life of Jesus, Mary and Joseph. Those same virtues can be practiced by every family in any country or culture. Family virtues are the fruit of a couple's love for God and for each other.

Duties of married life

The purpose of Matrimony is twofold: the mutual love and benefit of husband and wife, and the begetting and proper upbringing of children. These two purposes are inseparable. In addition, Matrimony is a sacred sign recalling the perpetual love of Christ and His Church.

Two persons act for Jesus in Matrimony, the man and woman who are receiving the sacrament. They give the sacrament of Matrimony to each other. The priest or deacon witnesses the sacrament and gives the couple God's blessing. The sign of Matrimony is the exchange of vows (important promises) to love and be loyal to one another for a lifetime. This is possible with God's help.

The duties for married couples are lifelong love and fidelity to each other and the begetting and proper rearing of children. Because of these God-given duties, *artificial birth control, abortion* and *divorce with remarriage* are sinful.

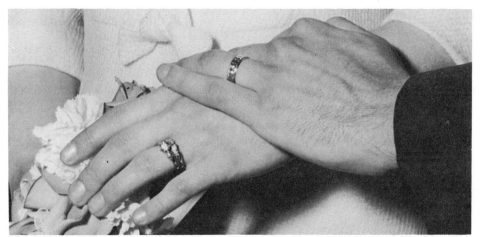

To receive the sacrament of Matrimony, a person must be baptized and not already joined to someone else by Matrimony. The person must obey the marriage laws of the Church. If the partner dies, the remaining spouse is free to receive the sacrament of Matrimony again. St. Paul says: "A wife is bound to her husband as long as he lives. If the husband dies, she is free to be married..." (1 Corinthians 7:39).

Mixed marriages between a Catholic and a non-Catholic are permitted by a dispensation or exception, but the Church does not encourage them. Catholics who enter mixed marriages must take great care to strengthen their faith, give good example and raise their children as Catholics. Because Matrimony is such a close union, the difference in religious beliefs can be a potential problem.

Marriage is a contract, a covenant, made before God, and it is unbreakable. This unbreakableness, called indissolubility, is for the good of the couple, their children and the whole of society. For a serious reason, the Church allows the partners of a valid marriage a separation, but without the right to marry again.

Divorce with remarriage is never permitted by the Church. The Church might permit a couple to obtain a civil divorce for legal reasons, but in God's eyes this couple is only separated. Neither may marry again while his or her spouse is still living. Adultery, sexual intercourse between a married person and someone who is not his or her married partner, is a serious sin. *Artificial birth control* profanes the sacrament of Matrimony as well. Because it is sinful, artificial birth control or contraception hinders the graces of God which are needed for a good and happy marriage. Natural methods of birth control for serious reasons are recognized by the Church because these do not directly block God's creative action. Catholics contemplating natural family planning should first seek the advice of a priest. In many dioceses, Natural Family Planning offices exist to guide couples.

Divorced Catholics and Catholics who have entered into invalid marriages are loved, too, by the Church and are encouraged to keep close to the practices of their Catholic Faith, especially the Sunday Mass. Divorced Catholics who have not remarried and are free from serious sin may also receive Holy Communion.

Church authorities may decide that an apparently valid marriage between two baptized persons can be declared null because of a fatal flaw. These flaws, unknown to one or both parties, or concealed by one or the other, make the marriage no marriage from the start. Church "tribunals" study each case and, where proper, give a Decree of Nullity—commonly called an annulment.

The sacrament of Matrimony is important to Jesus who instituted it, and to the Church who safeguards it. We are challenged to keep informed about the true meaning and worth of this sacred covenant.

Think about it

Marriage is not just a physical thing or a convenient arrangement. Marriage is a sacrament for which couples prepare with seriousness and reflection. Living together before marriage is seriously wrong and cheapens the total gift of one's self to another in this sacrament. To receive Matrimony worthily, it is necessary to be free from mortal sin, to know and understand the duties of married life, and to obey the laws of the Church concerning marriage. Couples can look to the model married couple: St. Joseph and his wife, Mary. To prepare well for this sacrament, they can practice virtue, especially chastity; pray for the wisdom to choose the right partner for this lifelong contract and receive the sacraments of Penance and Holy Eucharist often.

Evidence of Jesus in my life

Movie magazines and soap operas do not honestly portray the sacrament of Matrimony. Am I careful and courageous enough to avoid books, magazines and media that can confuse or distort my values?

Prayer

Jesus, Mary and Joseph, I entrust and consecrate
myself entirely to you—mind, heart and body.
Guard and defend me always from every sin.
May my mind be uplifted to heavenly things;
may my heart love God more and more;
my I avoid every evil occasion.
Keep me close to You, so that I may keep a watch
on my internal and external senses and in heaven
join the blessed company of the saints.

Servant of God,
Father James Alberione

All the Way Home

The screech of brakes, the shatter of glass, a heavy thud and then silence. The motorcyclist lay in the road by the tree that he had just hit, head on. A man from the nearby farmhouse heard the impact and came running. The farmer's son arrived moments later. "Call an ambulance and Father Nick," the older man shouted. "This boy is in bad condition." The ambulance wound its way down the dark country roads to the scene, but the priest, who was much closer, arrived first. He knelt next to the broken, bleeding youth and caught sight of a miraculous medal around his neck. Father took out his small kit and administered the Anointing of the

Sick. It seemed that the young victim was dead as the priest traced the Sign of the Cross with oil on his bleeding forehead and hands, reciting the prayers. After the sacrament was administered, the priest asked: "Do you hear me?" The priest called again even louder: "Can you hear me, son?" Slowly, the lifeless expression on the boy's face changed to recognition. "Yes," he answered softly. "Yes,...and thank you." He smiled, leaned his head back and closed his eyes. His whole being seemed to relax. He was now ready to go to his eternal home.

Unless we reflect on a story like the above, it is so easy to get lost in the events of every day and the here and now. How little we think of the afterlife, of eternity which lasts forever. But the infinite God has a global view of life and of death. He never for an instant loses sight of our goal. He has given us His sacramental help all through our earthly existence beginning with Baptism, then Penance, Eucharist and Confirmation. For many, there is the sacrament of Matrimony or Holy Orders. But when the Lord comes for us, when He calls us to our eternal home, or when through sickness or old age, there is the possibility that He might call us home soon, He gives us a sacrament to prepare the way. It is called the Anointing of the Sick.

The Anointing of the Sick is the sacrament by which Christ gives comfort and strength to the soul, and sometimes to the body, of someone who is dangerously ill due to sickness, injury or old age. The priest who acts for Jesus administers the Anointing of the Sick. The sacrament is made up of the anointing of the forehead and hands with blessed oils and the words. The blessed oil is called the oil of the sick. It stands for healing, chiefly spiritual healing, but also physical healing. The words of the sacrament of Anointing signify that we are asking the Lord to give His strength, His healing, His grace.

To receive this sacrament worthily, one should be in the state of grace. For this reason it is customary to receive the sacrament of Penance first unless one is unconscious. After confession the sick person receives the Anointing of the Sick, then the Holy Eucharist. The priest should be called even if a person is apparently dead because the Anointing and absolution can be given for some time after apparent death. If there is doubt about whether the Anointing of the Sick should be given to someone or not, call a priest and be sure.

A person should receive the Anointing of the Sick when he or she begins to be in danger of death due to sickness or old age. It is a good practice to ask the priest to visit sick members of the family in the case of serious illness, even though there is no apparent danger of death. Sick children, too, may receive this sacrament if they are old enough to be comforted by it.

The elderly who are in a weakened condition are also encouraged by the Church to receive the Anointing, even though no dangerous illness is present.

Some relatives of seriously ill persons at times can have a false compassion for them. They do not want to alarm the patient by calling a priest, and fear that the thought of imminent death might distress the dying person. But such a mentality is wrong. It is a serious duty and great charity to call a priest in time of serious illness.

The terms: the *last sacraments* or the *last rites* refer to those sacraments received by a person who is seriously ill. They include Penance, the Anointing of the Sick, and Viaticum (Holy Eucharist). With these sacraments, the Church prepares us for our journey back to God.

Think about it

So many thoughts have already passed through our minds today. Remembering as many of those thoughts as we can, would we consider them useful for eternity? How many of those thoughts would we want God to see? Would He be able to reward us for them? Studying about the sacrament that prepares people to meet God makes us evaluate the way we are living our lives. Are we running after that which is superficial, or even morally wrong? Then it does us good to consider that our life on earth does not end in the grave, but has a new beginning that will never end, in eternity. Some people take great care to establish a pension that will guarantee a long and ease-filled retirement. But few there are who are as equally caring for their "eternal retirement."

Caring spiritually for the sick

Have you ever visited a very sick person in the hospital when the priest was making a visit to anoint that person? Did you notice how the room was prepared? Whether this sacrament is received at home or in the hospital, make the following preparations. Prepare a table in the sickroom, and cover it with a linen cloth. On it place a crucifix, two candles, and some holy water. The priest administers the sacraments of Reconciliation and Eucharist if the patient is conscious. Then follows the Rite of Anointing.

This Rite differs from the Rite of Communion of the Sick which consists of a Eucharistic minister, deacon or priest bringing the Eucharist to a sick or elderly person who is not able to go to church. Such a visit, often made weekly in many parishes, is called a *sick call.*

A priest "makes a sick call" in this manner: he enters the house, gives everyone a greeting of peace, and then places the Blessed Sacrament on the table. All adore it. Then the priest sprinkles the sick person and the room with holy water, saying the prescribed prayer. The priest may then hear the sick person's confession. If sacramental confession is not part of the rite or if others are to receive Communion along with the sick person, the priest invites them to join in a penitential rite. A text from Scripture may then be read by one of those present or by the priest, who may explain the text. The Lord's Prayer follows. Then the priest distributes Holy Communion. A period of sacred silence may be observed. A concluding prayer and a blessing complete the Rite of Communion of the Sick.

At times deacons or Eucharistic ministers may visit the sick. Although they cannot celebrate the sacrament of Penance, they can distribute Holy Communion.

Think about it

Through the Anointing of the Sick, Jesus fortifies the sick person's soul with more grace and with the strength to resist temptations. Often temptations are strongest when one is physically weak. Jesus gives the sick person comfort to bear his or her sufferings bravely, and courage and consolation in the face of death. He cleanses the soul of venial sin and removes mortal sin, even forgotten ones, if the person wishes forgiveness but is unable to make his confession. The Lord remits at least some of the temporal punishment due to sin. Sometimes the sacrament also restores physical health, if that would be helpful for the sick person's salvation.

Evidence of Jesus in my life

Does it cross my mind each day that sooner or later the end of my life will come? Am I living today as if it were my last?

Prayer

Father, accept us all in the cross of Christ; accept the Church and humanity, the Church and the world.

Accept those who accept the cross; those who do not understand it and those who avoid it; those who do not accept it and those who fight in order to erase and uproot this sign from the land of the living.

Father, accept us all in the cross of Your Son! Accept each of us in the cross of Christ!

Disregarding everything that happens in man's heart, disregarding the fruits of his works and of the events of the modern world, accept man!

May the cross of Your Son remain as the sign of the acceptance of the prodigal son by the Father....

Pope John Paul II

Rules for Building a Happy Life

- The first three commandments regulate our relationship with God.

- The fourth commandment obliges us to obey lawful authority.

- The fifth commandment teaches the sacredness of human life.

- The sixth and ninth commandments safeguard purity of mind and actions.

- The seventh and tenth commandments govern the ownership and use of this world's goods.

- The eighth commandment requires us to be truthful in our words and actions.

Our God Is God

A lady in her fifties walked into a Catholic book and audiovisual center and approached one of the religious sisters who was serving the people. There was an earnestness in the woman's face as she whispered to sister: "I don't belong to any religion yet, but I see the need of having rules to regulate the way I live my life. Does the Catholic Church teach rules for right living?" "Why yes," sister responded. "First of all, the Church teaches the ten commandments." "I want to learn about those rules, those commandments," the lady said simply. And she selected two paperback books explaining the commandments.

What had motivated this woman who had been raised without religious principles to seek them? Even if no one had instructed her in the Faith, she sought religious instruction just the same. This points to a mysterious part of each and every human being called by Vatican Council II: "The secret core and sanctuary of a man" (Church in the Modern World, no. 16). That secret sanctuary is our own conscience.

Conscience is a practical judgment (decision) that something is right or wrong according to the law and will of God. Conscience is the echo of the Maker guiding us to recognize the moral implications of our thoughts, words and actions. To act according to our conscience, we realize we need to inform our conscience correctly. To have a correct conscience one first needs to know God's law (the natural law for all people, written down in the ten commandments and made more perfect by Jesus), the laws of the Church and also his or her particular duties as a Catholic. Then one's conscience will really express what is right or wrong in a particular situation.

Loving God first

The first three commandments of God reflect our proper relationship with Him. "I am the Lord your God:

1. You shall not have strange gods before me.

2. You shall not take the name of the Lord your God in vain.

3. Remember to keep holy the Sabbath day..." (Exodus 20).

Rules to be lived must be understood and applied to our own lives. Each of the ten commandments not only "fits" into our lives, but also will shape and mold us into Christians who use our time on earth to prepare for the heavenly reward.

The **first commandment** obliges us to love God above all things and adore Him alone. To adore God means to render Him the worship due Him as our Creator and Lord, avoiding the sins of idolatry and sacrilege. Idolatry means worshiping other persons or things in place of God. Exaggerated selfishness and secularism can also be an offense against the first commandment.

Sacrilege is the abuse of a person, place or thing consecrated to God and His service. Those who unjustly imprison priests and religious because of their allegiance to Christ commit the sin of sacrilege. Those who treat sacred places unworthily or desecrate the tabernacle commit a sacrilege. Devil worship is a serious offense against the first commandment.

Besides forbidding certain sins, the first commandment also requires positive obligations: that we worship God, that we talk to Him regularly in prayer. We should also venerate and seek the intercession of Mary, His Mother, and the saints.

His name is holy

The **second commandment** obliges us to always speak reverently of God, of the Blessed Virgin, of the angels and the saints. This commandment forbids profanity, perjury, blasphemy and cursing. Profanity is the irreverent use of the name of God, Christ or the saints through impatience, jest, surprise or habit. When the sixth grade CCD teacher in a particular parish informed the students that profanity, popularly called "swearing" is a sin, a boy raised his hand and asked shyly: "But Sister, how can swearing be wrong? Everybody in my family swears!" This sad fact could be true of a number of families, but that does not lessen the offense.

An *oath* is a declaration before God that what we say is true. It is lawful to take an oath because it is a guarantee of truth.

The conditions which make an oath lawful are:
—sufficient reason for taking an oath;
—conviction that we speak the truth;
—that the intention for taking the oath is not sinful.

Perjury is the calling upon God to bear witness to a lie. Perjury is also committed when, while under oath, one confirms with certainty something which is unknown or doubtful. Lying on the witness stand is perjury.

Blasphemy is any word, thought or action which shows contempt for God, the Blessed Virgin, the angels, saints or religion. Two conditions necessary for blasphemy to occur are: knowledge of God and the sacred; deliberate contempt for the same. To ridicule religion, to deliberately mock religious customs and rites, or that which pertains to our Faith, such as the priesthood and religious life, can be blasphemy. When mockeries of this nature are exploited through the media, the damage is incalculable. Cursing, also forbidden by this commandment, is the calling down of evil on some person, place or thing.

The taking of vows is also considered under the second commandment. A vow is a free and deliberate promise made to God by which a person binds himself under pain of sin to do something which is possible, morally good and better than its voluntary omission. The vows made most frequently are those of poverty, chastity and obedience taken by persons living in religious communities or consecrated to God.

The worship of our God

The **third commandment** requires that we keep the Lord's day holy. This commandment obliges us to worship God on Sundays and holy days of obligation. Sunday is set aside as a special day because of a tradition handed down from the Apostles which took its origin from the very day of Christ's resurrection. This day bears the name of the Lord's day or Sunday.

We keep the Lord's day holy by participating in the Eucharistic Celebration or Mass on Sundays and holy days of obligation. This obligation may also be fulfilled if necessary on the evening of the previous day. The rest of the day is made holy by abstaining from such work or business which impedes the worship to be rendered to God. This would include unnecessary shopping or heavy work. Our Sunday activities should not hinder the joy which is proper to the Lord's day, or the proper relaxation of mind and body. Some people must work on the Lord's day because their job requires it of them, but unnecessary work should be avoided.

Especially suited as Sunday activities which renew our soul and body are: reading a good book, doing works of charity, cultivating our cultural interests and wholesome recreation.

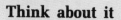

Think about it

God knows each of us better than we could ever know ourselves. Sometimes we think we know what we need and what is good for us. But God has our lasting happiness at heart. He has given us rules compatible with our human nature.

These rules require self-discipline of us, but we have a Model to imitate, Jesus, the Divine Teacher. Jesus not only lived the commandments given to Moses on Mount Sinai (see: Exodus 19:16-25; 20:1-17), but He excelled in the practice of each of them. Best of all, He gave us the motivation for keeping the commandments not fear but love. By His living and dying, Jesus gave the greatest glory to His Father in heaven. He taught us how to love and how to show that love.

Evidence of Jesus in my life

Is my life guided by the norms of morality which come from God, the ten commandments, or is it easy to detect in my words and attitudes that I make my own laws?

Prayer

Jesus, Divine Teacher, help us to pray with reverence the ten commandments which came from Your Father in heaven.

I am the Lord your God:

1. You shall not have strange gods before me.

2. You shall not take the name of the Lord your God in vain.

3. Remember to keep holy the Sabbath day.

4. Honor your father and your mother.

5. You shall not kill.

6. You shall not commit adultery.

7. You shall not steal.

8. You shall not bear false witness against your neighbor.

9. You shall not covet your neighbor's wife.

10. You shall not covet your neighbor's goods

(see: Exodus 20:1-17)

A Law and a Promise

The remaining seven commandments govern the way we live our lives and our relationship with others. The fourth commandment of God is:

"Honor your father and your mother..." (Exodus 20:12).

St. Paul explained to the Ephesians: "Children, obey your parents in the Lord, for that is what is expected of you." The fourth commandment is the first commandment to carry a promise with it. "Honor your father and your mother that it may go well with you and that you may have a long life on the earth" (Ephesians 6:1-3).

Parents have authority that comes from God Himself. Children, on the other hand, have the obligation to obey in everything that is not sinful and to care for their parents. To obey is good, but it is only the minimum. We can carry out an order or a request, but accompany it with complaints and criticism. This is not compatible with the "spirit" of the fourth commandment which forbids all disrespect, unkindness, stubbornness, spitefulness, complaints and disobedience toward our parents and lawful authorities.

Sometimes, the older we grow the more we thirst for independence, for being on our own. We envision adulthood as being free to guide our own life, to do precisely what we want, if we want, when we want. But is this realistic? No human being is totally independent. No human being can do only and always what he wants, not even the most wealthy or politically powerful person in the world. No one is autonomous. In our civilized society, for example, we need stores, schools, hospitals, vehicles of transportation, mail delivery and much more. These help us to satisfy our physical needs. And when we look at our parish Church, we realize that we even worship together in a praying community because God created us social beings. Only God is autonomous. Only God needs no one or nothing.

Children need their parents. Teenagers need their parents. This is not a sign of weakness or immaturity. To recognize this need is to be realistic. It is in accord with the fourth commandment and is pleasing to God. Children show their love and respect for their parents when they speak and act with gratitude, try to please them, readily accept corrections, seek advice in important decisions, patiently bear with their parents' faults, and pray for them.

Parents have duties toward their children, too. First of all, they must love their children, have their children baptized within the first few weeks after birth and provide for their material welfare. Parents must instruct their children and give them a Christian education, correct their bad habits and tendencies, train them by word and example in the practice of Christian virtue, and counsel and guide them in forming a correct moral conscience. You might think as a teenager that obeying is difficult, but as an adult you will find one thing more difficult, and that is having to give orders. It is much easier to obey than to require obedience of others.

Think about it

It is easy to more or less take for granted the home we come from and the parents God has given us. But when, as teenagers, you study about the fourth commandment, it awakens a new realization about love and respect. Your years at home will pass more quickly than you can imagine. You will be ready for adulthood if you take the responsibility for your teenage years now. Don't let time just slip by. Put your whole self into each and every day. Learn self-discipline by studying hard, being industrious in school, helpful at home, conscientious on the part-time job, generous in doing service, using your free time well. It is easy, instead, to waste time, spending hours listening to music or watching television. But by giving in to that kind of self-indulgence we do no justice to ourselves and we will accomplish little good with our lives.

Public duty

Besides our parents, the fourth commandment obliges us to respect and obey our teachers and lawful superiors, both civil and ecclesiastical, when they discharge their official duties in conformity with the law of God. Laws for public safety must be obeyed, even such ordinary laws as a traffic light, a stop sign, and signs posting the speed limit. It involves far more than receiving a traffic fine. It is a matter of conscience and obeying God's law. To disobey traffic laws is to endanger your life as well as the lives of others. To obey the fourth commandment, we should keep the laws because we see God's will in them, not for fear of penalty or punishment. If the civil law obliges or allows citizens to violate the law of God, we must refuse to obey. An example of this would be the 1973 *abortion decision* which has been the cause of the death of several million innocent children.

Employers must be just to their workers and workers must be just to their employers. As loyal citizens of our country we must respect civil authority, and obey just laws. That is, we must conscientiously fulfill all civil duties. The principal civil duties are to pay taxes, to defend one's country, to fulfill one's duty of voting, to work for and support laws which protect Christian morals and the common good.

Patriotism is the love for and allegiance to our country. Patriotism is loyalty and involves trying our best to be worthy citizens of our homeland. The day we begin to take our country for granted, that is when we have to ask ourselves if our virtue of patriotism is diminishing.

Even voting is considered under the fourth commandment. It is a sin to vote for an enemy of religion or of the national well-being because by voting for him, one voluntarily participates in the evil which such a person could do if he were elected. A pro-abortion or pro-choice candidate, for example, could do much harm. In our day, a key area to note when selecting candidates is human life issues. Selecting candidates who are openly and sincerely *pro-life* is essential. Candidates who are uncommitted or opposed to life would not be able to best serve the people for whom they are elected. Catholics must vote for people whose beliefs and programs are sincerely beneficial to everyone in such essential areas as *pro-life*. It could even be a sin not to vote if by not voting one were the cause of an incompetent or perverse candidate being elected.

Think about it

Living each day is simplified by moral guidelines given to us in the ten commandments. They are like the rudder that helps to steer the ship on its course. The practice of each commandment helps us to grow in the Christian life. Faith becomes alive and vital. The fourth commandment guides us in the practice of obedience to our parents and rightful authority. By it we learn to take the responsibility of our actions, to be just with everyone. We learn what it takes to be an upright citizen of our nation. Above all, we learn gratitude to God and to our families for all that we have been given.

Evidence of Jesus in my life

How do I show respect? Am I respectful of my parents, teachers, even young people my own age or younger? How often do I recall the presence of Jesus and act accordingly?

Prayer

Give me a strong faith, Lord, so that I can see Your hand at work everywhere.

Give me a strong will, Lord, to profit from everything I learn in order to become inseparable from You.

Give me a strong heart, Lord, to love Your Church more and more— that Church into which You have poured the fullness of Your love and Your truth.

Human Life Is Precious

We might know and be aware of the many Right to Life or Pro-life organizations so active throughout our nation. Perhaps our parents, relatives, neighbors as well as ourselves are actively involved in promoting the pro-life effort. Or perhaps we are aware of the movement but as yet we have not become directly involved. Whatever be our case, as we study the fifth commandment and apply it to our life and our world today, we deepen our understanding of the importance of being "pro-life" or "for life."

The fifth commandment of God is: "You shall not kill" (Exodus 20:13). Patient Job, the Old Testament man of suffering, wisely exclaimed: "In his hand is the soul of every living thing, and the life breath of all mankind" (Job 12:10). The Bible's first book, Genesis, as we recall from previous lessons, gives an account of creation in such a way that the singular importance of human beings is clearly emphasized. After God had created the earth and all that is in it, God created man in His own image (see: Genesis 1:26).

To say that we are made in God's image is a reminder that we human beings have intellects that can think, and wills that can make choices. Once created, from the moment of conception, our souls will never die. Human beings are precious because they are destined for eternal happiness with God forever. That is why we should keep reminding ourselves of the importance of our time on this earth. Because of God's gift to us of free will, He gives us the responsibility to choose our own destiny.

Think about it

The life of every human being is equally precious to God. There is no such thing as a "quality of human life" ethic in which some human beings are more "human" than others. All human beings are equally valuable to their Creator. He does not judge "worth" by the talents we possess, the money we have, the important positions of our parents, or our health. He sees right through all those things which are His gifts anyway. His glance penetrates to our very soul upon which is stamped "His image" (see: Genesis 1:27). Sometimes we might be tempted to become depressed because we are so ordinary. We imagine that we are lost in anonymity. When depressing thoughts of our own unimportance come to mind, we should remember that God has created a beautiful world for us to live in and a beautiful heaven to live for. He loves each of us individually. He died for each of us individually, and He will give each of us an eternal reward if we are faithful to Him.

The commandment that safeguards life

The fifth commandment commands us to take care of our own life and the lives of others. "You shall not kill" applies to all innocent human life, including that of the unborn child, who has the same right to life as any other human person. Abortion at any time after the child is conceived in the womb of his mother deprives the unborn of this basic right, and therefore it is murder.

Other crimes against human life and human dignity are any type of murder such as euthanasia or "mercy-killing," culpable suicide, torture, mutilation, or sterilization of the human body without a serious reason. (One serious reason would be a fibroid or malignant tumor that would have to be removed to insure the health of the individual.) Brainwashing, indecent living and working conditions, forced

imprisonment of innocent people, being deported from one's country, slavery, and the selling of men, women and children are also serious offences against the fifth commandment.

It is sinful to directly intend to shorten one's life, for example, by choosing to work under dangerous conditions in the hope of shortening one's own life. But a person may risk his or her life or health for a serious motive, such as, to save the life of another person. The famous "four chaplains" of the Second World War, a Catholic priest, two Protestant ministers and a Jewish rabbi, gave their life jackets to men stranded on the torpedoed *USS Dorchester*. The four chaplains, linked arm in arm, amid the frigid waters of the Arctic Sea, went down together. The three hundred survivors in rafts would remember forever the picture of those four men rejoicing that so many of their flock had "cheated" death, and

happy to offer themselves instead. History knows the four courageous chaplains as the Rev. George Lansing Fox, a Methodist minister from Vermont; Rabbi Alexander David Goode of Brooklyn, New York; Rev. Clark Vandersall Poling, a minister from Upstate New York; and Rev. John Patrick Washington, a Catholic priest from Newark, New Jersey. Deeply convinced of the sacredness of the lives of the men entrusted to their spiritual care, they forfeited their own lives for others.

It may be lawful to take the life of another person:

—to protect one's own life and possessions and those of one's neighbor from an unjust attacker, provided no other means of protection is effective;

—in fighting a just war;

—to execute just punishment for a crime, though many Catholic thinkers hold that capital punishment is not justified in our time.

Living up to our obligations

Our spiritual well-being is even more important than our physical well-being, because we are not destined for this life alone but for eternal life. Respect for the spiritual well-being of others involves an obligation to give good example both in our private and public life. The fifth commandment helps us to consider our obligation as Catholics to sincerely practice our religion, to practice self-restraint in the use of food and alcoholic beverages and to avoid chemical dependency on drugs.

If we fail to give good example, to show in our lives that Christ lives in us, we may be a source of *scandal* to others. Scandal is bad example. Some sources of scandal are: the use of improper and bad language; immoral films, TV and radio programs, and literature; immodest styles and the example of bad companions. We can fail against the fifth commandment also by quarreling and fighting, by giving in to anger, hatred, revenge, drunkenness, and the taking of harmful or dangerous drugs. This commandment also obliges us to use ordinary means (food, water, sleep, shelter, medical attention) to preserve our life. Extraordinary means, such as those which involve very great pain, expense, or other extreme difficulties, may not be obligatory. Church authorities may and should be consulted when there is a doubt as to whether a means is extraordinary or not.

A murder a minute

Our nation's number one killer is not war; the number one killer is abortion. In the nine wars and two hundred and ten years since 1775, there have been 667,286 American battle deaths. In 1972 alone, 600,000 babies were killed by abortion—more than a murder a minute for each of the 525,600 minutes in a year.

In *Human Life Review*, President Reagan stated: "...Since 1973, more than fifteen million unborn children have had their lives snuffed out. That is over ten times the number of Americans lost in all our nation's wars."

Legal abortion in California alone has killed more babies than the number of American servicemen killed in the Vietnam, Korean, Spanish, Mexican, 1812 and Revolutionary wars put together. In war, the medical corps saved lives; in

abortion, the medical profession kills lives. Aborted babies receive no Purple Hearts, no "taps," no Memorial Day.

If we are concerned about war, it is only logical that we be concerned about abortion. Pope John Paul II said: "The killing of unborn life is not a legitimate means of natural family planning." Pope Paul VI said: "All human life must be absolutely respected; in fact, abortion and euthanasia are murder."

As members of the Catholic Church, we have a sacred moral code to live up to and people watch us to see if we live up to what we profess. As Pope Paul VI once so candidly remarked: "The world waits to see a saint passing by."

Prejudice

Respect for human life means respect for our own life and the lives of all. This is because all people, created in the image and likeness of God, have been redeemed by Christ and are destined for eternal life. Opposed to the fifth commandment is prejudice of every kind. Webster defines prejudice as: "a preconceived judgment or opinion." And again: "an irrational attitude of hostility directed against an individual, a group, a race, or their supposed characteristics."

Prejudice is founded on ignorance and is bred by a subtle kind of superior attitude. Prejudice causes us to fail to see human beings as individuals, as creatures of God. Instead, we label people by race, ethnic origin, religious affiliation, occupation, or even by some physical condition, such as a deformity. If we call people names, and systematically exclude them from our friendship be it among our relatives, or at school, work or in the neighborhood, we might honestly have to face the fact that we are prejudiced.

Think about it

Sometimes the prejudices of children have been learned from adults, perhaps even from the immediate family. Or perhaps young people learn prejudice from their environment, their friends at school or their neighbors. When we deliberately try to exclude and ignore people, when we look down on them and take secret delight in hurting them, it is time to stop and examine our consciences on the fifth commandment. Then we must seek Jesus' forgiveness in the sacrament of Reconciliation. Remember what was said of Jesus: "He has done everything well..." (Mark 7:37). If we want to be true imitators of Jesus, then these words must also be true of us.

If we find, on the other hand, that we have been the object of prejudice, then we can look to the Divine Teacher's example of patience and loving forgiveness of His enemies. He even called Judas, His betrayer, "friend" (see: Matthew 26:50). Think of it! Jesus is God. How much we can learn from Him.

Evidence of Jesus in my life

Do I refuse to permit prejudice of any kind in my life? Do I avoid all name calling or any other form of prejudice as totally against the teachings and life of Jesus?

Prayer

O Mother of all peoples, Mary, you know of their sufferings and their hopes, you feel in a motherly way all the struggles between good and evil, between light and darkness, that shake the world. Accept our cry addressed in the Holy Spirit directly to your heart and embrace with the love of the Mother and handmaid of the Lord the people who are most awaiting this embrace, and at the same time the people whose trust you also particularly expect. Take under your motherly protection the whole human family, which we entrust to you with affectionate joy, O Mother. May the time of peace and freedom, the time of truth, justice and hope, approach for everyone.

—*Pope John Paul II*

Preserving "His Image" in Us

Teenage saints canonized by the Church practiced virtue in a heroic manner. Dominic Savio wanted at all costs to attend Don Bosco's school for boys in Turin, Italy. The boy asked: "Don Bosco, will you teach me how to become a saint?" The kindly priest smiled and said: "Why not, Dominic? You be the cloth and I will be the tailor. I will 'weave' you into a beautiful garment for Christ." At that time, Dominic was eleven years old. With cheerful determination, he obeyed the "tailor" and applied himself to loving Jesus and growing close to Him. His health began to deteriorate, and after three short years the boy was dead, but through prayer and effort he had become a spiritual "success."

We can learn many good lessons from every saint, but as we focus on the sixth and ninth commandments, Sts. Dominic Savio and Maria Goretti have a particular message. Dominic Savio avoided immoral talk, bad pictures and occasions that seemed like fun but would possibly lead to sin. Dominic worked hard at guarding purity in every day situations.

She chose to "really live"

On a summer day in 1902, a twelve-year-old girl named Maria was left at home to take care of her baby sister and to clean the house. Her mother, Assunta Goretti, along with Maria's brothers, had gone with a neighbor, Mr. Serenelli, to continue the harvesting. Ever since Maria's father had died, there was always so much more work to be done.

It was unbearably hot that day. But all of central Italy is hot during the summer. After everyone had left the poor farmhouse, Maria collected the dishes and began her chores. Then she realized that not everyone had gone. Alexander, the eighteen-year-old son of Mr. Serenelli, had remained behind. Alexander's eyes followed Maria as she worked. He was pensive for a moment. He said at last, "Maria, I have a shirt to be mended. I need it for Mass tomorrow. Fix it for me this afternoon. It's on my bed."

Maria knew that Alexander never went to Mass and she suspected something. But as soon as she finished the dishes, she got the shirt and settled herself on the porch, with her baby sister, Theresa, sleeping peacefully beside her.

My mother is right, Maria thought. There is something bothering me. But how can I tell her? Alexander threatened to kill me. Maria broke out in a cold, clammy sweat and her heart pounded furiously. I've got to tell her, she thought. I've got to—but how? He has approached me twice already, and sooner or later he is bound to overpower me. I feel so weak and helpless. O my God, give me the strength and courage I need never to commit sin. My Lord, I am so afraid.

Then, suddenly, what she feared most happened. Alexander stood beside her. "I won't take 'no' for an answer," he shouted. "Give in or I'll kill you."

"No, no! I won't. It's a sin. God forbids it. Alexander, you will go to hell if you do it!" His anger turned into rage. He poised a knife over her. There was a moment of silence. One moment in which to choose life or death, sin or martyrdom. With superhuman courage, Maria chose God.

"No, Alexander, I won't!"

Again and again Alexander plunged the knife into the body of his helpless victim. Maria made no attempt to ward off his blows. Then she lost consciousness. The sight of the blood sobered the boy somewhat and he fled from the room.

When Maria came to, she was in an agony of pain. She dragged herself through the pool of her own blood toward the kitchen door. Slowly, she unbolted it and made a feeble effort to call for help.

As soon as Alexander heard her voice, he ran back to the kitchen, grabbed her by the throat and stabbed her clear through six more times. Then he barred himself in his bedroom.

Writhing in pain, Maria lay in that condition for another hour before anyone came back to the house. It was Mr. Serenelli who found her. He called frantically to Maria's mother, who was still working out in the fields. Maria's mother collapsed from the shock, but kind neighbor women immediately set to work.

Maria's clothes were saturated with blood that had congealed and the material had to be cut off piece by piece. All the while, Maria's lips remained sealed. She would not

reveal the name of her assailant. Finally, Mamma Assunta managed to get some information.

"It was Alexander," Maria whispered.

"But why?" asked Mamma.

"Because I refused to sin."

It was enough. Mamma Assunta pried no further. Maria was taken to a hospital in nearby Nettuno. But her ordeal was not over. The surgeons decided to operate with no anesthesia. They found fourteen wounds. Her intestines were torn, her lungs pierced completely through and her heart grazed. She passed the night in sheer torture.

The next morning when the priest brought Holy Communion, Maria said: "I pardon Alexander. I desire that someday he may join me in heaven."

Maria was now near death. She had blood poisoning; she was hemorrhaging internally; her respiration was failing. Shortly after three o'clock on July 2, 1902, Maria surrendered her soul to God.

And what of Alexander Serenelli whose evil deed was born from his obsession with pornographic literature? He served a prison term of thirty-five years and returned a changed man. On Christmas Eve, 1937, he went to beg pardon of Mamma Assunta.

"Maria forgave you, Alexander," the heroic mother replied. "How could I possibly refuse to?" The next day Alexander went to the parish church. There, before receiving Holy Communion, he suddenly turned and said to the astonished congregation:

"I have sinned deeply. I murdered an innocent girl who loved virtue more than life. May God forgive me! I beg your pardon."

Today the incorrupt body of St. Maria Goretti lies enshrined in a glass urn in the church at Nettuno.

What can we learn from Maria Goretti? She was neither simple-minded nor ignorant. She consciously and freely gave her life rather than lose the priceless treasure of her virginity. Was Maria's life wasted because she chose virtue over sin? Death over life? No, Maria chose the better part; she knew what it meant to *really live*. She chose God's way, the only way.

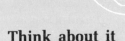

Think about it

Our Catholic Faith challenges us to live up to Christian moral values given to us by the Divine Teacher Himself in the Sermon on the Mount (see: Matthew, chapters 5-8). Jesus taught purity in our actions and words. But He also taught purity of mind, that is, purity in thoughts and desires. But being pure and remaining pure takes grace and will power obtained through prayer and frequent reception of the sacraments. It also takes instruction. We are required to learn and study about the sixth and ninth commandments. These commandments are the safeguards of purity. Our study should lead us to the conviction of the importance and worth of this virtue. We pray for the grace that comes from the Divine Teacher to be true to the sixth and ninth commandments.

Two important rules

The sixth commandment of God is this: "You shall not commit adultery" (Exodus 20:14). The sixth commandment obliges us to be pure and modest in behavior both when alone and with others. The ninth commandment of God is this: "You shall not covet your neighbor's wife" (Exodus 2:17). The ninth commandment obliges us to be pure in thoughts and desires.

We study the sixth and ninth commandments together because both concern the virtue of purity: external purity (how we speak and act) in the sixth commandment, and internal purity (how we think, imagine and desire) in the ninth commandment. Purity is sometimes called chastity. It is the virtue by which we properly regulate our use of the sexual acts according to our state in life. To be pure according to our state in life means to keep the sixth and ninth commandments if we are married, single, young, middle-aged or old. Priests and religious take a vow of celibacy or chastity. They freely choose to give up their right to marry and form their own family in order to give themselves totally to Jesus and to serving the spiritual needs of His people. They must keep the sixth and ninth commandments which serve as a strong foundation for keeping the vow.

Married people have the particular graces of the sacrament of Matrimony. They, too, must be chaste according to their state in life, not misusing their married rights, and being respectful with each other. Modesty is that virtue which inclines us to guard our senses so as to avoid possible temptations. It also causes us to refrain from whatever might incite others to sin. This includes dressing and acting decently, avoiding tight or scant clothing and being modest.

Temptations against the sixth and ninth commandments are not sinful in themselves. However, we must reject impure thoughts, imaginings and desires at once, ignore them or try to distract ourselves by other thoughts and by prayer. They only become sinful when we willingly indulge and give in to them.

Safeguarding morality

Adultery is a serious offense against God as well as one's married partner. Homosexual activity and masturbation are gravely forbidden because they violate and mock the divine plan: "...Male and female he created them" (Genesis 1:27).

The Church condemns all forms of artificial birth control such as pills, drugs, or mechanical devices, because these are against the natural purpose of married love, that is, the transmission or giving of life. If serious reasons warrant the limitation of births, Catholics may practice natural family planning. Couples may consult a priest or Catholic Natural Family Planning groups.

Being pro-life, living pro-life, is our challenge. It begins with the way we act with ourselves. We must treat our body as a sacred thing because it truly is, due to the fact that God lives within us by grace. The principal means for practicing this virtue of purity are frequent Holy Communion and a great devotion to the Blessed Virgin. Keeping pure takes personal effort, too. We must watch our actions, conversations, etc., and avoid, as much as possible, all dangerous occasions.

Zaire's martyr of purity

In Kinshasha, Zaire, on the feast of the Assumption, 1985, Pope John Paul II proclaimed a twenty-five-year old nun as black Africa's first woman martyr of the Roman Catholic Church and publicly forgave the soldier who killed her.

On the eighth day of Pope John Paul's twelve day African pilgrimage, Sister Marie Clementine Anwarite Nengapeta was beatified before sixty thousand people at an outdoor Mass. The Holy Father, in referring to the *Assumption* of the Blessed Virgin Mary, said: "On this happy occasion when we celebrate the glory of the Virgin Mary, the Church solemnly proclaims her daughter, *Marie Clementine Anwarite*, as blessed, a martyr of the faith among you."

Sister Anwarite's killer, Colonel Pierre Openge Olombe, at the age of twenty-six, had led a rebel group that overran the Catholic mission station in eastern Zaire on November 30, 1964. Olombe, helped by his men, clubbed and bayoneted Blessed Marie Clementine Anwarite to death after she fought off his attempt to rape her. Diverting from his prepared text, the Holy Father referred to the young martyr's repentant, convicted killer with these words:

"I myself, in the name of the whole Church, forgive him with all my heart."

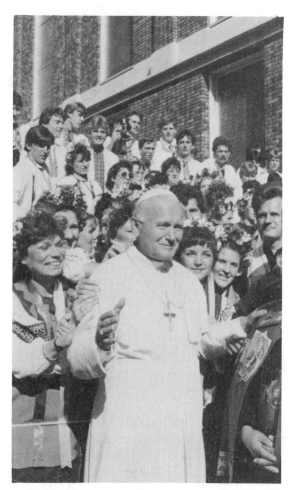

Think about it

Living a clean, chaste life takes prayer and effort. We should avoid idleness, bad company, unbridled curiosity, excessive eating and drinking which lead people to seek continual bodily satisfaction, immodest dress, immoral reading and other media; suggestive music and obscene talk.

Being pure has a price. At the beginning of this chapter, we briefly considered two saints who were willing to pay the price: St. Dominic Savio and St. Maria Goretti. We know that if we are faithful to God's laws as they were, we too will receive the reward. Each of us might like to ask ourselves: Am I willing to make the effort and thus to pay the price?

Evidence of Jesus in my life

When someone tells a "dirty" joke, makes an off-color remark about someone, or something similar, how do I react? Am I willing to risk being laughed at, and say that such behavior is wrong? Or do I prefer popularity to the peace of conscience that Jesus gives?

Prayer

Lord, give me what I need to become what I want to be.
My relationship with You,
Your Mother and Your Church is so weak.
There is so much in my life that does not resemble You
or Your Vicar, the Pope.
You and he wouldn't think and talk
the way I sometimes do.
Help me. My life is Your gift.
Inspire me to spend it well for You.
I will ask Your Mother, Mary, to help me.

Rule of "Give and Take"

Two more commandments are best studied together, the seventh and tenth. The seventh commandment has to do with actions; the tenth commandment with our thoughts. The seventh commandment is: "You shall not steal" (Exodus 20:15). The tenth commandment is: "You shall not covet your neighbor's goods" (Exodus 20:17). These commandments oblige us to be honest and to respect all that concerns the possessions of others. Large department stores report thousands of dollars in loss annually, and their reports show steady loss increases. This makes us reflect to see if such a fact might be an indication of a rather widespread problem in society: that is, a disregard for the seventh and tenth commandments.

A tour of any city neighborhood, not just after dark, but even in the daytime, reveals an atmosphere of fear. People in homes and apartments are not secure enough with a lock on each door. Some have added padlocks and one or more chains. When God's rules, His ten commandments, are set aside, life in civilized society becomes tense and fearful. Many innocent people suffer.

The slogan: "it pays to be honest," has a great deal of truth to it.

The seventh commandment forbids stealing and robbery, unjust acquisition of goods and reckless destruction of what belongs to others. The tenth commandment forbids even the desire to take or to keep our neighbor's goods. Stealing can be mortally sinful if the thing stolen is of considerable value (otherwise it is a venial sin). Stealing something of small value can be mortally sinful if the owner is poor, and thus suffers great injury. Some thefts today are drug-related. People trapped in chemical dependency find the costly habit hard to control. They therefore lie, cheat and steal for the money they need for the next "fix." No matter why we steal, we are bound to be sorry for our sins, and confess them. We are obliged to adhere to the law of restitution, which means we must return stolen goods or their value in money to the owner. Or, if the owner is dead, to his family. If neither the owner nor the family of the owner can be discovered, the goods or their value are to be given to the poor or to charitable causes.

171

Breaking the seventh and tenth commandments is an injustice to God and to our neighbor. We learn from these commandments how to keep our "wants" under control. We cannot have everything we see or think about. Our desire to possess must be guided by right reason. Sometimes we have to review in our minds the commandments and how they apply to our lives. These rules were not given by God to be crafted to our own wants. They are norms on which to build our moral life. In fact, our very life and all the good things we possess are God's gifts to us.

Dishonesty is "self-cheating"

All of us have heard about the card game "Solitare." Since Solitare is played alone, cheating does not make too much sense. It means to cheat against ourselves. Some people play the game of life that way. They cheat here and there, little realizing that they are cheating against themselves. This is because all of our thoughts, desires, words and actions will be waiting for us at the judgment.

Some more subtle forms of stealing are: cheating the consumer as to the exact worth of a machine or object being sold; hiding a defect in that object; doing poor work and repairs through negligence; repairing machinery and changing parts unnecessarily; charging a price that deserves a better job; acquiring money or positions by dishonest means; performing operations on people who do not need them; making false insurance claims; "fixing" games in sports so that certain teams win or lose.

A bribe is an offering of money or other valuable objects with the intention to corrupt. Bribery, obviously, is wrong and can be seriously wrong. It is wrong to offer bribes and wrong to accept them. A bribe is "pay" for privileges that are

not our right to offer or receive. A bribe is like a hunter's snare. Once we fall in, we become more and more tangled in the net. Bribes have a beginning. That beginning is the acceptance of the first one, but to stop taking them is much more difficult.

Gambling, too, is regulated by the seventh commandment. Gambling is the staking of money or valuables on a future event or on a game of chance, the result of which is unknown. Gambling in itself can be an amusement, and it is not against Catholic moral standards if played fairly and honestly and with moderation. However, gambling can also become a sin, even a mortal sin, if it leads one to excesses such as dishonesty, and great loss of money, risking the needs of the family and even of society.

Unjustly damaging the property of others is also forbidden by the seventh commandment. Property means houses, lawns and belongings. To damage public property by defacing it with graffiti or by destroying it is equally wrong.

Human beings have a right to private ownership. This right, bestowed on a person by the Creator, provides the means for his livelihood, growth and progress. But the principle of private ownership does not justify the overabundance of some and the extreme poverty of others. No one is justified in keeping for his exclusive use what he does not need when others lack necessities. The employer's attitude should be one of equity or fairness. This means justice with charity, thus assuring his workers just wages, proper and dignified working conditions and reasonable safety on the job. Workers have the duty to

produce good work, to take reasonable care of the employer's property, to avoid damaging working materials through carelessness and to occupy the working hours fully and well.

When employers and employees have a mutual respect for each other, are conscientious and fair, a climate of goodness and trust is created. Such a situation is the result of faith in God and the realization that none of us is independent. We need each other and, above all, we need God, who is a just Judge, and our common Father.

Workers are permitted to strike when their rights are violated, lawful contracts are ignored or other serious difficulties arise. The strike, however, can be used only after all other means to solve the difficulties have produced negative results. Moreover, a strike must be conducted in a fair and peaceful manner, avoiding all forms of violence. And the gain expected from a strike must be greater than the losses sustained by going on strike.

Think about it

We may consider that there are two kinds of basic attitudes among people. Some individuals try to take either by honest means or dishonest means whatever they can as they go through life. Other individuals give what they can, lend what they can, help wherever they can. They work conscientiously for their earnings and do the best with what they have. If we think about it, we realize that there are many more honest people than dishonest ones. Honesty, it has been said, is the best policy. Honesty is God's policy.

Evidence of Jesus in my life

Am I trying to acquire *conscientiousness* every day? Do I have the habit of looking back after completing a task, and examining how well I did it? Is *honesty* one of my basic attitudes?

Prayer

Lord, teach me to be generous.
Teach me to serve You as You deserve:
To give without counting the cost,
To fight without heeding the wounds,
To toil without looking for rest,
To work without asking for a reward—
Except the reward of knowing
That I am doing Your will.
St Ignatius of Loyola

The Commandment of Truth

Truth is the opposite of a lie. A lie is something said which we know or suspect to be untrue. A lie is usually said for the purpose of deceiving others. By the eighth commandment we are obliged to be truthful and to interpret in the best possible way the actions of others. The eighth commandment is: "You shall not bear false witness against your neighbor" (Exodus 20:16). St. Paul said to the first Christians: "Put on the new nature, created after the likeness of God in true righteousness and holiness" (Ephesians 4:24).

The eighth commandment guards our thoughts and interpretations about our neighbor's character, words and actions. This commandment also governs the way we speak about everyone. We are challenged to examine ourselves on our speech in relationship to the individual dignity and worth of each human being. The principle is this: every person has the right to be respected by other persons. Sins against the person's right to respect are rash judgment, detraction, slander (also called calumny), and talebearing.

Rash judgment is believing, without sufficient reason, something harmful to another's character. Rash judgment is wrong because it causes us to think less good of another person and this is opposed to charity.

Detraction is making known, without good reason, the hidden faults of others. One is allowed to tell the faults of another when it is necessary to make them known to his parents or superiors, so that the faults may be corrected and the wrongdoer prevented from greater sin. If a person is convicted as a criminal, making known his faults is not detraction, because the person no longer has esteem in this matter. However, it is more charitable not to speak of them. Detraction is often the result of jealousy.

But even lower on the "rung" of the ladder of faults against truth are slander and talebearing. To slander is to lie about a person, injuring his or her good name. If we have the misfortune to commit the sins of detraction or slander, we must intend to repair and make up for our hurtful words. It is necessary, as far as is possible, to carefully weigh our words and our motives before we speak.

Talebearing is telling persons what others have said about them, especially if the things said are evil. It is wrong because it gives rise to anger, hatred, and ill-will, and is often the cause of greater sins.

One day a woman went to seek advice from the holy and witty St. Philip Neri, a sixteenth century priest in Rome. Many people liked to go to St. Philip for the sacrament of Penance or confession because he had such a wonderful way of helping them not only repent of their sins but to grow in the love of God.

This particular lady had a problem which could also be called a *bad habit*. She talked about people. She told tales and lies about them. The woman realized she was not only hurting others, but, above all, she was offending God when she did this. She wanted to correct herself so she told good Father Philip.

The priest listened intently as she confessed her sins and applied the remedy. "Do this," Father said. "Take a chicken and go out on the side of the road and pluck all its feathers. Toss the feathers into the air and watch the wind scatter them. Wait a few hours. Then go back outside and gather up all those feathers."

"But, Father," the woman gasped, "that is impossible! I will never be able to find all the feathers!"

"So it is, my good lady, with the reputation of others. We are doing just that when we lie and gossip about them. We are sending their reputation to the four corners of the earth and we will never be able to undo the harm we have done."

Think about it

The eighth commandment regulates the use of our tongue. St. James handles the role of our tongue in an unforgettable way in chapter three of his New Testament book of the Bible which says:

"The tongue is a little member and boasts of great things. How great a forest is set ablaze by a small fire!

"And the tongue is a fire. The tongue is an unrighteous world among our members, staining the whole body, setting on fire the cycle of nature, and set on fire by hell. For every kind of beast and bird, of reptile and sea creature, can be tamed and has been tamed by humankind, but no human being can tame the tongue—a restless evil, full of deadly poison. With it we bless the Lord and Father, and with it we curse men, who are made in the likeness of God. From the same mouth come blessing and cursing. My brethren, this ought not to be so."

(James 3:5-10)

Going over these words, we begin to see the responsibility we have for the good use of our tongue.

Confidentiality, or the keeping of secrets, is also the subject of the eighth commandment. When are we obliged to keep secrets? We are obliged to keep secrets when we have promised to do so, when our office or position requires it, or when the good of others demands it. Keeping secrets is an obligation and it goes back to the control of our tongue that St. James spoke of.

Media and truth

Society needs information in order to make right decisions, and well-informed citizens contribute to their personal progress as well as the common good. The producers and directors of media have an obligation to be truthful in program presentation as well as advertising. This presupposes sufficient instruction, diligent and accurate researching, factual scripts free of bias.

The eighth commandment also touches the viewers, the individuals in the living room watching television or the movie at the local theatre. They cannot control what is written or produced, but they can control what they watch on television, the movies they go to see and, if they are parents, what their families watch. This is called *selectivity*. Just because a certain program is on television does not automatically mean it is suitable for children and many times adults.

Viewers have an obligation to train themselves to sift out bias and prejudice, to detect the sensational in order to reject it. Listeners and viewers have the duty to accept the truth, and to reject what is opposed to it. They do this by reacting to what is being presented to them. They should show dissatisfaction with distortions, omissions, biased reporting of facts and events out of context. They should also expect that mistakes be corrected and that events should not be underplayed or exaggerated.

The spreading of truthful information that recognizes human dignity, and is for the benefit of all, is the sure and just way to form public opinion.

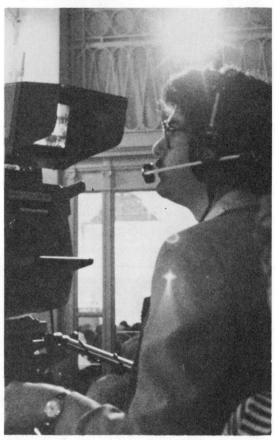

Think about it

Truth is the conveying of reality—what is. Jesus, on trial for His life, before Pilate said:
"For this I was born,
  and for this I have come into the world,
to bear witness to the truth. Every one who is of the truth
  hears my voice" (John 18:37).

Sad to say, Pontius Pilate retorted: "What is truth?" (John 18:38). But our answer is far different. The Divine Teacher has given us the gift of faith, of belief in Him as God, who is Himself our Truth (see: John 14:6). We pledge to the divine King our love for truth and our desire with His help to live always in the truth.

Evidence of Jesus in my life

Do I control my curiosity and my tongue? Am I honest with my words? Do I avoid exaggeration and insinuation? Do I see Jesus in the people around me and respect His presence in them?

Prayer

O God, to communicate Your love to people,
You sent Your only Son, Jesus Christ,
into the world and made Him our Master,
the Way and Truth and Life of humanity.
Grant that the media of social communication—
press, films, radio, television and records—
may always be used for Your glory
and the good of souls.
Raise up vocations for this
multi-media apostolate, and inspire
all people of good will to contribute
with prayer, action and offerings, so that
through these means the Church may preach
the Gospel to all peoples. Amen.

Servant of God
Father James Alberione

Catholic Precepts and Practice

- Love is the motivating force behind the living of Christian morality.

- Jesus taught love of God and neighbor in the parable of the *Good Samaritan*.

- The Church gives us laws called precepts. Catholics practice *fasting* and *abstinence* to grow closer to God.

- Religious life is a special call to imitate Jesus through the vows of poverty, chastity, obedience and community life.

- *Indulgences* and *sacramentals* help us toward our goal of heaven.

From Law to Love

During His whole time on this earth, Jesus was teaching. He taught with His words and His actions. In the Gospels, the Divine Teacher explained to the crowds and to all of us what would be expected of someone who wants to be a follower of Jesus. What He taught was based on a single word, too freely used today, yet often not really understood. The word is "love."

Jesus' concept of love, based on the Old Testament books of Deuteronomy 6:4f., and Leviticus 19:18, is called the *Great Commandment*.

"You shall love the Lord your God with all your heart, with all your soul, and with all your mind...and your neighbor as yourself."

(see: Matthew 22:37, 39)

The Divine Teacher did everything totally. When we read the Gospels and study what He said and did, we realize that His way of life embraces every part of us. To be a true Christian involves our thoughts, words, actions and attitudes. We cannot split our thoughts, words, our actions and attitudes from our commitment to Jesus. How do we know if our way of living is truly Christian?

First of all, we examine our *thoughts, words, actions* and *attitudes* on the ten commandments. And then we dare to take a further step beyond the basic moral code of right living to the realm of love. Jesus the Teacher went far beyond the minimum requirements for right living. He expected the "maximum" of Himself and of everyone who considers himself or herself a follower of the Teacher. We have duties towards God, self and neighbor as our study of the ten commandments has shown us. But what makes Christian morality so appealing, even though difficult, is the motivating force behind it all: *love.*

We are to love God with our whole being. We are to love others as Jesus loves us, and because God loves them and wants us to do the same. Christian morality is living in a way worthy of our dignity as human beings and God's adopted children.

Think about it

We should remind ourselves often of the *supernatural* realities of life. "Why am I important?" we can ask. We know the answer: "because I am God's adopted child." Through Baptism and the other sacraments, we share in God's life. This makes us both *keepers* and *sharers* of a treasure. Our Catholic Faith is to be shared with others, first of all, by the good example we give in living it.

Evangelization is the spreading of the Gospel, that is, the Good News about what Jesus has done for us, what He expects of us, and what He promises us. Jesus said to us: "I am the light of the world" (John 8:12). "You are the light of the world" (Matthew 5:14). Jesus called us the "light of the world" because He wants us to lead good lives, and give the truth to others. Spiritually, we can either do the "least" or the "most." If we take up the challenge to make the maximum effort to become close to Jesus, or holy, then we are imitating the saints. For example, St. Paul was able to say: "Be imitators of me as I am of Christ" (1 Corinthians 11:1).

Faith in action

When we let Jesus' love penetrate us and make the living of our Catholic Faith a top priority in our lives, the Divine Teacher fills us with a faith-dimension that gives a new depth to our very selves. We come to the realization that to live our faith takes prayer, generosity and self-discipline. We live our Faith by studying our religion, by making frequent acts of faith, and by showing faith in good actions. After reading and thinking about this, we might honestly have to admit that we have to improve on several points in our lives. The important thing is to *begin*. It might call for some changes. But with the strength that comes from prayer, we will have the grace to make the changes that we should.

We live our Faith by avoiding whatever endangers it, such as bad companions, the reading of bad literature, pride of mind and heart. These can lead to denial of some or all the truths of Faith, or indifference in the practice of our Faith. Precautions are essential and require a prayerful maturity of us. We will not necessarily see many others our own age living a fervent Catholic life. So what will we do? Let mediocrity or even bad living win us? That looks like the easy way...the way to freedom and happiness. But it is not. Jesus' way is the only way to happiness that lasts.

Roger Staubach, who played professional football for the Dallas Cowboys, recently said this about his Catholic Faith:

"I don't think anyone should be ashamed of his or her religion or fail to practice it at any age. I have always felt that if you stick to your beliefs and you are willing to stand up for your religion, you will be respected in the long run and will not be laughed at. I feel I have been successful and able to succeed in whatever I am doing because of my strong faith. I do share my testimony with others, but try not to be overbearing.

"I do let people know how important my Faith is to me and that it does affect my everyday life. I feel I would be rejecting God's love and blessings if I didn't use my opportunities to the utmost, to talk about my Faith, and why it is precious to me. To enjoy something beautiful like this to the fullest, you must share it."

Think about it

We show our faith in action by bringing the Gospel spirit into every aspect of our life, especially into our relations with our fellow human beings. This is how we witness to Christ and contribute to extending the kingdom of God and building a more human world. As Roger Staubach says, "I feel I would be rejecting God's love and blessings if I didn't use my opportunities to the utmost, to talk about my Faith and why it is precious to me."

Evidence of Jesus in my life

Do I have a humble attitude when it comes to my Catholic Faith? Am I conscious of trying to be a more convinced and committed Catholic? Do I examine my conscience daily on my thoughts, words, actions and attitudes?

Prayer

O Jesus,
help me to overcome selfishness
and to replace it with generosity.
Give me the desire
to be close to You
and to care about what You
care about—
the salvation of all the people
in the world.
Help me to be strong
in time of temptation
and keep evil far from me.

And Who Is My Neighbor?

The Divine Teacher had a story to tell—a story with a moral called a *parable*. In order to grasp what the Master was teaching, the listeners had to understand that a Samaritan was a person of Jewish origins whose family had inter-married with pagans. The Samaritans lived apart from the Jews in little towns (see: Luke 9:51-56). The Jews thought themselves superior to the Samaritans who had not remained true to Hebrew laws and customs. The Jewish priests and Levites, men close to the Temple of Jerusalem, were thought to be holy. Imagine the impact of Jesus' story, told to a Jewish audience.

"And who is my neighbor?" (Luke 10:29), a Hebrew lawyer asked Jesus. The Master's reply has become one of the best-loved stories of all time, the parable of the *Good Samaritan*. Jesus wanted His listeners to recognize the sharp contrast between someone who is a neighbor and someone who isn't. Jesus' listeners sat on the hillside, and clung to every word. But they did not realize the way the story would unfold. The one least expected to be a good neighbor proved to be an *excellent* neighbor, and those who should have excelled in charity did not.

The road from Jerusalem to Jericho was dusty and hot. Most of the time, it was lonely and deserted. Travelers were easy prey for thieves. The hazards of traveling that road were well known. Many had been robbed, beaten and even killed. The Lord told it this way:

"A man was going down from Jerusalem to Jericho, and he fell among robbers, who stripped him and beat him, and departed, leaving him half dead. Now by chance a priest was going down that road; and when he saw him he passed by on the other side. So likewise a Levite, when he came to the place and saw him, passed by on the other side. But a Samaritan, as he journeyed, came to where he was; and when he saw him, he had compassion, and went to him and bound up his wounds, pouring on oil and wine; then he set him on his own beast and brought him to an inn, and took care of him. And the next day he took out two denarii and gave them to the innkeeper, saying, 'Take care of him;

and whatever more you spend, I will repay you when I come back.' Which of these three, do you think, proved neighbor to the man who fell among the robbers?" The Lawyer said, "The one who showed mercy on him." And Jesus said to him, "Go and do likewise" (Luke 10:30-37).

Think about it

The hero of Jesus' parable was the person considered most likely not to be. The man was from Samaria, a rather unlikely location, some would say, to find someone "good." But *good* he was! And what was the measure of his goodness? The way he treated others. Re-read the story carefully. Ponder the choices. The priest had the choice of helping a beaten, unconscious man lying on the road. He did not. A Levite, a member of the priestly Hebrew tribe of Levi, saw the crumpled, bleeding heap on the road, and he, too, passed by. The Samaritan, instead, interrupted his own journey, cared for the injured man, took him to a travelers' inn, paid for his upkeep, and promised to stop in on the return trip to take care of added expenses, if any. The Samaritan did the most, not the least, for a complete stranger who might not even have been conscious enough to say "thank you." The Samaritan was willing to inconvenience himself to the maximum. And he did it willingly and cheerfully. What a lesson! Jesus said simply, "Go and do the same."

How can we "go and do the same"?

We most likely will never travel the road from Jerusalem to Jericho. How can we, today, ever have the opportunity to imitate the Good Samaritan of Jesus' parable? By practicing the *spiritual* and *corporal works of mercy.*

The *spiritual works of mercy* have to do with the spiritual part of human beings, our souls. They are: to counsel the doubtful, to instruct the ignorant, to admonish the sinner, to comfort the sorrowful, to forgive injuries, to bear wrongs patiently, to pray for the living and the dead.

The *corporal works of mercy* have to do with the material part of human beings, our bodily needs. They are: to feed the hungry, to give drink to the thirsty, to clothe the naked, to shelter the homeless, to visit the sick, to visit the imprisoned, to bury the dead.

If we look closely at each of the works of mercy and think about the spirit of love that those works should inspire in us, we come to the realization of what the Divine Teacher is asking. Each of us is invited to become the Good Samaritan in a variety of ways and according to what is possible for us. As just one example, we can practice a spiritual work of mercy right now by saying a prayer for someone whom we know needs it. We can also pray for those who have shown special love for us, like our family, relatives, neighbors and friends.

Each of the works of mercy brings a two-fold gift: relief to a fellow suffering human being and joy to the one who practices the work of mercy. The Good Samaritan put others' needs before his own. This takes generosity and when generosity is present, selfishness dwindles. The Good Samaritan of Jesus' story was a happy man because he was generous.

Think about it

Jesus, the Teacher, who knows human nature thoroughly, was *total* in His teachings. How could people practice works of mercy if they lacked inner convictions and correct mental attitudes? In Matthew's Gospel, chapter five, the Lord proposes eight ways to be happy. These teach us to long for our heavenly homeland and to view everything that comes into our lives, even sad events, from a supernatural perspective. What we suffer with patience and love on this earth will be rewarded by Jesus in heaven.

Evidence of Jesus in my life

What have I done today to make someone a little happier? To ease a burden? To be of encouragement? Am I willing to try to acquire that goodness of the "Good Samaritan"?

Prayer

Let us recite often, as a prayer, Jesus' eight beatitudes:

"Blessed are the poor in spirit, for theirs is the kingdom of heaven.

"Blessed are those who mourn, for they shall be comforted.

"Blessed are the meek, for they shall inherit the earth.

"Blessed are those who hunger and thirst for righteousness, for they shall be satisfied.

"Blessed are the merciful, for they shall obtain mercy.

"Blessed are the pure in heart, for they shall see God.

"Blessed are the peacemakers, for they shall be called sons of God.

"Blessed are those who are persecuted for righteousness' sake, for theirs is the kingdom of heaven.

"Blessed are you when men revile you and persecute you and utter all kinds of evil against you falsely on my account. Rejoice and be glad, for your reward is great in heaven, for so men persecuted the prophets who were before you" (Matthew 5:3-12).

Why Does the Church Make Laws?

The Church makes laws for one reason only, and that is to help us reach our goal of heaven. It is no small matter that we reach our eternal homeland. This, in fact, is why we have been created. Jesus left us His Church to guide us to the goal. The Catholic Church was given the right to make laws from Jesus who said to the Apostles, the first bishops of the Church:

"Whatever you bind on earth shall be bound in heaven" (see: Matthew 16:19).

The Church's right to make laws is exercised by the Pope and bishops united with him. The Pope has complete, supreme, ordinary and immediate jurisdiction over the universal Church. Laws which affect the universal Church may also be made by a general council of bishops united with the Pope.

Rules and duties

Our membership in Jesus' Church implies some duties on our part. Some of the special duties of Catholics are called the *Precepts of the Church*. The precepts or rules of the Church help us to mold our spiritual life as followers of Jesus. When we make a genuine effort to practice our Faith, the Lord will walk through life with us. He will give us the strength to live Christian values, which are His values, in a world that preaches the opposite.

Rules, as we know, are to be kept. The Precepts of the Church are special duties which we, as Catholics, are expected to obey and fulfill. They are:

1. To keep holy the day of the Lord's resurrection: to worship God by participating in Mass every Sunday and Holy Day of Obligation: to avoid those activities that would hinder renewal of soul and body.

2. To lead a sacramental life: to receive Holy Communion frequently and the sacrament of Penance regularly—

—to receive the sacrament of Penance at least once a year (annual confession is obligatory only if serious sin is involved).

—minimally, to receive Holy Communion at least once a year, usually between the first Sunday of Lent and Trinity Sunday. For a good reason, the precept may be fulfilled at another time during the year.

3. To study Catholic teaching in preparation for the sacrament of Confirmation, to be confirmed, and then to continue to study and advance the cause of Christ.

4. To observe the marriage laws of the Church: to give religious training (by example and word) to one's children; to use parish schools and religious education programs.

5. To strengthen and support the Church: one's own parish community and parish priests; the worldwide Church and the Holy Father.

6. To do penance, including abstaining from meat and fasting from food on the appointed days.

7. To join in the missionary spirit and apostolate of the Church.

Evidence of Jesus in my life

In examining the Precepts of the Church, do I find in myself the conscious awareness of wanting to obey them? Do I pray, asking the Divine Teacher to help me keep these important rules that come from His Church?

Prayer

O God, Shepherd and Ruler of
  all the faithful,
look with favor upon Your
  servant, the Pope,
whom You have appointed Pastor
  of Your Church.
Grant that by word and example,
he may assist those whom he serves
so that the shepherd and the flock
entrusted to his care may together
attain everlasting life.
We ask this through Jesus Christ,
  our Lord. Amen.

Facing Our Obligations

Some people might not appreciate the word: *obligation*. It has the ringing sound of finality about it. *Obligation* implies *duty*. We have all found, no doubt, that as we grow up, we acquire more duties. Usually, adults have more serious and more numerous obligations than teenagers. But when it comes to the living and practicing of our Catholic Faith, our duties begin when we acquire the use of reason, around seven years old.

A serious duty of Catholics is to worship God on Sunday (or Saturday evening) at the Eucharistic Celebration or Mass. The Catholic who, through negligence, misses Mass on a Sunday (or Saturday evening) or holy day of obligation (or the preceding evening) commits a mortal sin. Realizing the importance of the Mass, some Catholics participate more than once a week, even daily, in the Eucharistic Celebration.

We cannot easily exempt ourselves from Sunday Mass. The graces that we need to live fervent Catholic lives come to us through the Mass.

Besides Sunday Mass, the Church also invites us to assist at Mass on certain days called holy days. Holy days were instituted to recall to our minds the sacred mysteries of our Catholic Faith. Holy days also recall important events in the lives of Jesus, Mary and the saints.

There are six holy days of obligation in the United States:

—January 1, the Solemnity of Mary, Mother of God

—Ascension of our Lord (forty days after Easter)

—August 15, the Assumption of the Blessed Virgin Mary

—November 1, All Saints' Day

—December 8, the Immaculate Conception of the Blessed Virgin Mary

—December 25, Christmas Day.

On the first day of every new year, we honor *Mary, the Mother of God* and our mother. As Jesus hung on the cross, He gave His mother to us in the person of St. John (see: John 19:26ff.). Our journey through this life is marked with trials and challenges of every kind. In order to use our time well for God, we need His mother to guide and protect us.

Forty days after Easter, we celebrate the *Ascension of our Lord,* when Jesus went back to heaven, never to die again (See: Acts 1:9). There He waits for us. He has our place marked out for us if we are faithful now.

On August 15, we celebrate the *Assumption of the Blessed Virgin Mary.* Assumption means "assumed" or "taken up." Mary was taken up, body and soul, into heaven. Because of her divine motherhood, Mary's body was never touched by the corruption of the grave. We meditate this marvelous privilege of our Lady every time we recite the fourth glorious mystery of the rosary.

All Saints' Day, November 1, is a day set aside to honor all the people who ever walked this earth and are now enjoying God's glory forever in heaven. Some saints have their own feast day. But how many countless more there are in heaven, including perhaps our own deceased loved ones. On this joyful day, we honor all God's saints by participating in the Eucharistic Celebration.

Another important feast of the Blessed Virgin Mary is the *Immaculate Conception,* celebrated on December 8. We give praise to God for Mary's privilege of being conceived without original sin. As the Mother of God's Son, Mary is the "sinless one."

December 25, *Christmas Day,* we celebrate the birth of Jesus—the Savior of the world. How important these celebrations are in our rich Catholic tradition. (It is important to note that the great feast of the Lord's resurrection is not listed among the holy days because Easter is always celebrated on Sunday, just as the first Easter was [see: John 20:1]).

Think about it

How many people live to be one hundred years old? Do you think you will? Even if you do live to be one hundred or more, how long is that in relation to eternity? What is a hundred years when compared with *forever*? Should we then spend some time preparing for heaven which will last forever? The best way is to live up to our obligations as Catholics, not sorrowfully or ungenerously but cheerfully. We can think about Saint Paul's words to the first Christians:

"Rejoice in the Lord always! I say it again. Rejoice! Everyone should see how unselfish you are. The Lord is near. Dismiss all anxiety from your minds. Present your needs to God in every form of prayer and in petitions full of gratitude. Then God's own peace, which is beyond all understanding, will stand guard over your hearts and minds, in Christ Jesus" (Philippians 4:7).

The important things

In considering our life in the perspective of eternity, we begin to set our priorities correctly. We give prominence to the spiritual. With our spiritual priorities in mind, we would not try to exempt ourselves from our Sunday obligation.

Some of those who are exempted from assisting at Sunday or holy day Mass are:

—the sick and those who must care for them;

—those who live a great distance from a Catholic church;

—those who have an urgent work (policeman, fireman, nurse on duty, etc.);

—those hampered by temporary difficulties such as weather (an elderly person in a snowstorm, or in very cold weather).

Anyone may freely consult a priest about his or her particular situation, and is encouraged to do so.

Penance is also part of our Catholic tradition. Penance is called *self-denial*, too. The Church invites us to willingly give up good things

for a higher motive—to strengthen us on our journey to heaven. When we voluntarily deny ourself something we like to eat or watch on television, we make a *sacrifice*. For example, a particular mother who loved chocolate candy, "gave it up" as a sacrifice for the intention that her teenage daughter would stop going around with bad companions. We practice penance, in other words, for spiritual motives, especially to draw closer to God and to ask God for graces for ourselves and others. The three shepherd children of Fatima in Portugal were invited by Our Lady of Fatima to pray and do penance for sinners. Mary told the children, during one of the times she appeared to them, "Many souls go to hell because they have no one to pray for them."

Certain penances, however, are not just suggested. They are required by the Church. Fasting is required of all Catholics who have reached the age of 18 but are not yet 59. In the United States, the only fast days are Ash Wednesday and Good Friday. A fast day is a day in which only one full meal is taken. The other two meals should not together equal a full meal. Eating between meals is not permitted, but liquids, including milk and fruit juices, are allowed.

Catholics are also obliged by the law of abstinence which means refraining from meat, and soups and gravies made from meat, on certain "days of abstinence" stipulated by the Church. The days for abstinence from meat in the United States are Ash Wednesday, the Fridays of Lent, and Good Friday. Catholics 14 years of age and over are obliged to keep this law.

Think about it

The Church has instituted fast days so that we Christians may learn to set our sights on God, and the destiny and goal of our life here on earth by denying our body. This is to follow the example of Jesus, who fasted and was tempted (see: Matthew 4:1-2). *Fasting* and *abstinence* are good for us.

Fasting and *abstinence* are not the only penances required of Catholics. We are to do more penances of our own choosing especially on Fridays throughout the year, since Jesus gave His life for us on a Friday, and during Lent, when we recall what the Lord suffered for us.

Evidence of Jesus in my life

My religious obligations are important. More important still for me is the maturity and generosity with which I face these obligations. How can I improve in the keeping of my obligations?

Prayer

Jesus, Divine Teacher,
the television commercials try to convince me
that I am the center of the universe
and that my needs are all that matter.
You lived a completely different kind of life—
a life of *giving*, not of *receiving*.
We all have our choice: to be *generous* or *selfish*.
Give me the grace to be strong in the face of
my own human weakness
and to willingly deny myself little things
so that I may acquire strength of character
that leads me closer and closer
to imitation of You.

What a Religious Vocation Is

The walks of life in which Christians may grow close to God and love their neighbor are: priesthood, the religious life, married life and the single life. As we form and deepen our Christian mentality, we become more and more convinced of the necessity to make the most out of our lives. We reflect that life itself is a vocation and a calling to use our time well for God.

Because human life is so precious, we can understand that the Divine Teacher offers us paths of life by which we can constantly grow closer to Him and do good to our neighbor. "Neighbor," of course, is any human being other than ourselves. The important thing is to pray daily, asking the Lord to direct our lives. We ask Him to show Himself in our lives, to be our "Way, our Truth and our Life" (John 14:6). He has a plan for each of us. He has a particular road for us to follow...a vocation, or calling, to do His will. We can be faithful to His will for us if we pray and ask it of the Lord constantly.

Religious life—a vocation

We realize that life itself is a vocation to be lived to the fullest. We also know that there are various walks in life. But what is the meaning of the word, *vocation.* A vocation is God's calling of a person to a particular way of life, especially the priesthood or religious life. Religious life is a special way of following Jesus. "Religious" are persons who make the vows of chastity, obedience and poverty in a

religious community. With these three vows or sacred promises, religious give up something and receive something.

The vow of chastity requires of religious to give up their right to form their own family. They become members of a community of religious who are their "family in Christ." Their hearts are further enriched by their love for and dedication to all those entrusted to their apostolic care for the love of Christ.

Through the vow of obedience, religious freely give up the right to do *what* they please *when* they please. They obey the set of rules (called *constitutions)* approved for their congregation. They obey superiors whom they see as God's representatives. By freely giving up their own will, with supernatural

dedication, they can strive to imitate closely Jesus who came to this earth to do His Father's will (see: John 12:49-50).

Religious poverty is the name of a promise or vow made by religious in which they renounce the ownership of the goods of this earth, and share things in common so that they will find their "treasure" in heaven (see: Matthew 19:16-22).

The vows of chastity, obedience and poverty are called the *evangelical counsels. Evangelical* means based on the Gospels. The vows are called *counsels* because unlike the ten commandments which all must obey, the counsels are invitations to do something more than the ordinary for the love of Christ. The religious life is a calling offered to whomever the Divine Master chooses.

Each vocation involves a call from God and acceptance on the part of the one who has been chosen. The Lord makes His voice heard in many ways, some of them quite ordinary. For example, we might see happy, fervent priests and religious brothers and sisters and want to know more about religious life. We might make more effort to pray fervently and spend some time daily in prayer before the Blessed Sacrament. One who is considering following a vocation should receive the sacraments of Reconciliation and Eucharist regularly and well, and gradually realize a desire to know more about religious life.

Secular Institutes and *Societies of Apostolic Life* are also special ways of following Jesus, similar in a number of ways to traditional religious life. A vocation to either manner of life is also a special calling with its own laws and spirit.

Think about it

Religious vows, called evangelical counsels, are meant to free the mind and heart of the religious so that he or she can love God entirely and serve His people *full time*. This life is a kind of foretaste of the way we will live in heaven. Religious priests, brothers and sisters should be the happiest people in this world! Why? Because the purpose of the life they choose is to give glory to God and to seek personal sanctification or holiness by imitating the life of Jesus. Each religious has to take seriously, as we all should, Jesus' own words: "You, therefore, must be perfect as your heavenly Father is perfect" (Matthew 5:48). Naturally, the religious life has crosses, too, but with prayer comes the strength to live Jesus words: "If any man would come after me, let him deny himself and take up his cross and follow me" (Matthew 16:24).

How did religious life begin?

To search out the roots of religious life, is to go back to Sacred Scripture, and most especially to the words and examples of Jesus, the Divine Teacher. To the rich young man Jesus said:

"If you would be perfect, go, sell what you possess and give to the poor, and you will have treasure in heaven; and come, and follow me."

(Matthew 19:21)

In every era of the twenty centuries since the Church's foundation, men and women have felt the call to imitate Christ in a particular manner. Some have become monks, hermits, or cloistered religious. Other religious serve God in a variety of apostolates. An *apostolate* is the carrying out of one or more of the spiritual or corporal works of mercy by a religious congregation. The purpose of any apostolate is always to make Christ better known, loved and served in the world. Some apostolates are nursing, teaching, evangelizing with the media and social work.

Many religious congregations and orders flourish in Jesus' Church, each with a rich heritage of spirituality given to the institute by the Founder. These religious live the vows of poverty, chastity, and obedience in common, according to their constitutions. *Community life,* an essential part of religious life, is the religious community's serene living together. It means sharing the same life of prayer, labor, the same food, accommodations and schedule, united in a common ideal.

Some religious priests, brothers and sisters become missionaries and lead self-sacrificing lives in parts of our own country where Catholic priests and religious are few. Others go to mission lands, laboring to bring the presence of Jesus and His Church to strangers whom the missionaries love in the Lord's name.

Not every priest is called a religious. Only those priests who belong to a religious congregation or order are called religious. Priests who do not belong to a religious congregation are called diocesan priests or parish priests because they are dedicated to ministering to the People of God in parishes. They are united in a diocese under a bishop. Every brother and sister is called a religious because each belongs to a religious congregation.

Religious priests receive the sacrament of Holy Orders, but religious life itself does not have a "special" sacrament. Religious make public profession of three vows of poverty, chastity and obedience in imitation of Jesus. Religious also promise to serve the Church by their dedication to the particular apostolic labors to which their religious congregation is dedicated.

Think about it

Religious life only makes sense from a *super*-natural point of view, not from the natural level. Religious put their faith and trust in Jesus, in the hope of eternal life with Him.

The Divine Teacher promised to faithful religious priests, brothers and sisters that:

"There is no one who has left house or wife or brothers or parents or children, for the sake of the kingdom of God, who will not receive manifold more in this time, and in the age to come eternal life."

(Luke 18:29-30)

Evidence of Jesus in my life

Have I ever stopped to consider the possibility of a religious vocation for me? Do I pray, asking the Divine Teacher for the grace to know and follow my vocation in life?

Prayer

Heavenly Father, I believe in Your wisdom and love.
I believe You created me for heaven,
marked out for me the way to reach it,
and await me there to give me the reward
of the faithful servant.
Give my light and show me this way.
Grant me the strength to follow it generously.
I beg this of You, through Jesus Christ Your Son
and through Mary my Queen and Mother.
At the moment of death,
may I be able to say with St. Paul:
"I have finished the course.
I have fought the good fight.
Now there is laid up for me the crown of the just."

Servant of God
Father James Alberione

Further Sharing in His Life

From the Divine Teacher's treasury of grace we Catholics are given the opportunity to partake of the wealth of *merits* the Lord won for us on Calvary. The Church takes away the *temporal punishment* due to sin by giving to us grace from the infinite satisfaction that Jesus made for sin (see: Romans 5:15-21; 1 Timothy 2:5-6; 1 John 2:1-2). This is the purpose of *indulgences* of which there are two kinds: *plenary* and *partial.*

A *plenary indulgence* is the removal of all the punishment, called temporal punishment, a person would have had to suffer in purgatory for sins already forgiven. A *partial indulgence* is the shortening or lessening of some of the temporal punishment due to forgiven sin. It can be acquired more than once a day.

Spiritual wealth of indulgences

We might wonder why we would have *temporal punishment* to pay for sins already forgiven. We have this "punishment" for forgiven sins because of the seriousness and evil of sin. We also have a debt to "pay" because of the infinite majesty of the One offended, God. Indulgences may be acquired for ourselves and for the souls in purgatory. A plenary indulgence can be acquired only once a day, unless at the point of death. In addition to performing the work to which the indulgence is attached, three conditions must be met to gain a plenary indulgence: "sacramental confession, Eucharistic Communion and prayer for the intentions of the Supreme Pontiff. It is further required that all attachment to sin, even venial sin, be absent" (Apostolic Constitution On Indulgences, no. 7). If the requirements for a plenary indulgence are not fulfilled, the indulgence will be only partial.

The faithful who use with devotion an object of piety (crucifix, cross, rosary, scapular or medal) properly blessed by any priest, can acquire a partial indulgence. For example, to pray with fervor on a blessed rosary will bring us the graces and blessings of Jesus through our Lady and a partial indulgence as well.

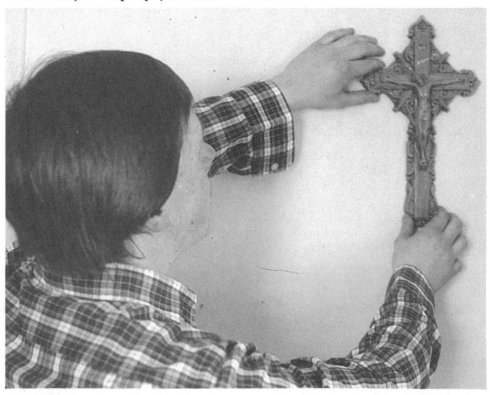

Think about it

The way Jesus lived on this earth and the way He died prove that He never did things by *half measures*. He wants us to be with Him forever, and He gives us every help. The Divine Giver opens His Church's "treasury" for each one of us. That treasury also includes the priceless value before God of the prayers and good works of His Mother Mary, and all the saints. They followed in the footsteps of Jesus, the Lord. By His grace the saints have sanctified their lives and fulfilled the mission entrusted to them by the Father.

Indulgences help us to make up for our sins. They also encourage us to perform prayerful acts. Some of these are participating in the Eucharistic Celebration, saying the rosary, reciting short prayers, called *aspirations*, as well as acts of penitence and charity.

What are sacramentals?

Another opportunity we have of growing closer to God is the reverent use of *sacramentals*. *Sacramentals* are holy things or actions with which the Church asks God to grant us favors, especially spiritual ones. Scripture speaks of how God told the Chosen People to use material things such as ashes and water in the Old Law (see: John 3:14-15; Numbers 19:1-22; Numbers 21:4-9). Sacramentals obtain favors from God through the prayers and devotion of God's People offered for those who make use of them, and because of the devotion they inspire.

One of the best known sacramentals is the blessing given by a priest (at the end of Mass, for example), or by a bishop, or the Pope. Every Wednesday, thousands of people from all over the world gather in St. Peter's Square at the Vatican to recite the *Angelus* at noon with the Holy Father, followed by his blessing.

Also called sacramentals are blessed devotional objects commonly used among Catholics. Some of these are: rosaries, relics, medals, crucifixes, scapulars, pictures of Jesus, Mary, the saints, ashes, palms and candles.

The rosary beads are "prayer beads" which, when blessed are enriched with indulgences for reciting the prescribed prayers. These beads are used to recite the "Gospel prayer" made up of Our Father's, Hail Mary's and Glory's, in which we think about important events in the lives of Jesus and Mary (see Prayer pages at the back of this text for instruction on how to say the rosary).

A *scapular* is two small pieces of cloth, fastened by strings, and worn around the neck in front and in back. The most common scapular honors Mary as Our Lady of Mount Carmel. A scapular medal may be worn in place of a scapular.

Another common sacramental is *holy water*. Did you ever wonder why we bless ourselves with holy water as we walk into church? We make the sign of the cross with holy water upon entering and leaving church to remind ourselves of our baptismal commitment and promises. If used with sincere dispositions, holy water can remove venial sin and fortify us against spiritual and physical temptations and dangers.

A first-class *relic* is a piece of a saint's bone or other particle of his body. A second-class *relic* is a piece of clothing or some other object which has been touched to the body of a saint.

Candles on the altar at Mass or votive candles lit by people of faith for special intentions, witness to our devotion to Jesus who is light and life with His grace. *Blessed ashes* are used especially on Ash Wednesday, the first day of Lent. A cross is traced with ashes on our forehead as a reminder to live a good life and do penance because one day we will die.

Sacramentals are not sacraments. They differ from sacraments in this manner: the sacraments give grace directly through the actions of Jesus, while sacramentals bring us grace through the intercession of the Church.

Think about it

Sacramentals are reminders for each of us that we are *Catholics*, and as Catholics, have taken on the commitment and the challenge to work for heaven. We look at a crucifix hanging on our wall and we remember that Jesus died for each of us and what a price He paid for our sins. We see a statue of Mary on our table or a framed picture of her on the wall. We are reminded that she is in heaven now, body and soul, with her Son. She will intercede with Him, as our good mother, and keep us close to Jesus.

When we kneel in church or at home in front of our favorite statue of Jesus, Mary or a saint, and say a prayer, we do not pray to the religious statues and pictures themselves. Instead, we pray to the person in heaven whom the statue or picture represents. If we pray with faith, our prayer will be heard and heeded according to the Lord's will.

Evidence of Jesus in my life

Am I conscious of the helps that I as a Catholic have? Indulgences and sacramentals, for example? Will I make myself more aware of the opportunities to acquire indulgences? Will I use sacramentals with devotion?

Prayer

Jesus, Divine Teacher, I have been given
a great treasure, my Catholic Faith.
You have "outdone" Yourself in offering me every help
on my earthly journey.
The next time I feel "down on myself" and think
that I am not worth anything, I will look
at a crucifix and thank You,
or I will take my rosary from my pocket
and say it with love to honor Your Mother.

Conclusion

Confirmation Is Initiation

By now you have realized that your text is nothing more than an *introduction* into the teachings of our Catholic Faith.

You have spent this time preparing to receive the sacrament of *Confirmation* which requires that you radiate your Faith to all whom you meet. Certainly, this sounds good on a printed page or in a book. But to *live* the teachings of the book is a work that takes a lifetime. And it is a work that requires love, as we learned from the Good Samaritan (see: Luke 10:25-37). What is meant here, of course, is Christian love which involves generous self-giving, fairness, thoughtfulness, honesty and much more. Perhaps the word "love" is summarized best by the word: *integrity.*

In your study this year, you should have recognized a vital fact. Each one of the lessons on the truths of our Faith, the ten commandments, the seven sacraments and Catholic practices only taught the *essentials.* The lessons have left to your mature sense of responsibility the obligation to deepen your knowledge by profound study in each of those areas as we go through life. The third Precept (or rule) of the Church, we recall, is:

"To study Catholic teaching in preparation for the sacrament of Confirmation, to be confirmed, *and then to continue to study and advance the cause of Christ."*

Think about it

Some people may have developed an erroneous concept that the sacrament of *Confirmation* is like *graduation*. In other words, once we receive this great sacrament, we are "done" with our Faith. Some seem to say: "There is nothing more to learn; it is no longer necessary to think about my Faith, to learn more about my Faith, to *practice* my Faith." Such people may not even feel obliged to fulfill their Sunday obligation of participating in the Eucharistic Celebration or Mass.

But *Confirmation* is not *graduation*. Confirmation, instead, is *initiation* into the mature Christian life. The Holy Spirit, who is God, is present in your heart, in a powerful manner. He wants you to let Him work in you, to fashion you into the likeness of Jesus. And when you feel weak, afraid to do God's will and cowardly in His service, you know what you have to do. You have to pray. Ask the Holy Spirit: Come into my soul. Make me what I should be. Keep me close to Jesus. Help me to put my Faith in the "front lines" where it should be.

Our Catholic Faith is the pearl of great price Jesus speaks of in Matthew's Gospel (see: Matthew 13:46). The Faith can be thought of as a lamp that lights up the darkness of your life when doubts, troubles, illness and disappointments come. Jesus said:

"One who lights a lamp does not put it in the cellar or under a bushel basket, but rather on a lampstand, so that they who come in may see the light."

(Luke 11:33)

The four Gospels contain many treasures of spiritual nourishment. How wise you would be to read a few paragraphs from the New Testament every day. The *Gospels* especially, which form part of the New Testament, contain the life and teachings of Jesus. Every day we should ask Jesus the Teacher, through His Holy Spirit, for an increase in faith. "The apostles said to the Lord, 'Increase our faith,' and he answered: 'If you had faith the size of a mustard seed, you could say to this sycamore, "Be uprooted and transplanted into the sea," and it would obey you'" (Luke 17:5-6).

Perhaps you may have seen a mustard seed encased in a transparent medallion and worn around the neck. How tiny that mustard seed is. Yet, to impress each one of us about the power of faith, Jesus compared the Apostles' faith to that tiny mustard seed. He has given us all the help we need to make our own faith grow. Out of respect and love for us, Jesus has given us a free will. Let us ask Him to help us use it well. Ask often, as the Apostles did: "Increase our faith." And He will....

Evidence of Jesus in my life

In an effort to make my faith grow, am I frequently making short "acts of faith"? Do I ask the Divine Teacher to increase my faith? May I never tire of asking.

Prayer

O Divine Holy Spirit, eternal love of the Father
and of the Son, I adore You, I thank You,
I love You, and I ask You pardon for all the times
I have offended You....
Descend with many graces during the holy ordination
of bishops and priests,
during the consecration of men and women religious,
during the reception of Confirmation by all the faithful;
be light, sanctity and zeal.
To You, O Spirit of Truth, I consecrate my mind,
imagination and memory; enlighten me.
May I know Jesus Christ our Master and
understand His Gospel and the teaching of Holy Church.
Increase in me the gifts of wisdom, knowledge,
understanding and counsel.
To You, O sanctifying Spirit, I consecrate my will.
Guide me in Your will,
sustain me in the observance of the commandments,
in the fulfillment of my duties.
Grant me the gifts of fortitude and holy fear of God.
To You, O life-giving Spirit, I consecrate my heart.
Guard and increase the divine life in me.
Grant me the gift of piety. Amen.

Servant of God,
Father James Alberione

PRAYERS

THE APOSTLES' CREED

I believe in God, the Father Almighty, Creator of heaven and earth. I believe in Jesus Christ, His only Son, our Lord. He was conceived by the power of the Holy Spirit and born of the Virgin Mary. He suffered under Pontius Pilate, was crucified, died, and was buried. He descended to the dead. On the third day He rose again. He ascended into heaven, and is seated at the right hand of the Father. He will come again to judge the living and the dead. I believe in the Holy Spirit, the holy catholic Church, the communion of saints, the forgiveness of sins, the resurrection of the body, and life everlasting.

AN ACT OF FAITH

O my God, I firmly believe that You are one God in three Divine Persons, Father, Son, and Holy Spirit; I believe that Your Divine Son became man and died for our sins, and that He will come to judge the living and the dead. I believe these and all the truths which the holy Catholic Church teaches, because You have revealed them, who can neither deceive nor be deceived.

AN ACT OF HOPE

O my God, relying on Your infinite goodness and promises, I hope to obtain pardon of my sins, the help of Your grace, and life everlasting, through the merits of Jesus Christ, my Lord and Redeemer.

THE SIGN OF THE CROSS

In the name of the Father, and of the Son, and of the Holy Spirit. Amen.

THE LORD'S PRAYER

Our Father, who art in heaven, hallowed be Thy name; Thy kingdom come; Thy will be done on earth as it is in heaven. Give us this day our daily bread; and forgive us our trespasses as we forgive those who trespass against us; and lead us not into temptation, but deliver us from evil. Amen.

THE HAIL MARY

Hail, Mary, full of grace! the Lord is with you. Blessed are you among women, and blessed is the fruit of your womb, Jesus. Holy Mary, Mother of God, pray for us sinners, now and at the hour of our death. Amen.

GLORY TO THE FATHER

Glory to the Father, and to the Son, and to the Holy Spirit: as it was in the beginning, is now, and will be for ever. Amen.

AN ACT OF LOVE

O my God, I love You above all things, with my whole heart and soul, because You are all good and worthy of all love. I love my neighbor as myself for the love of You. I forgive all who have injured me, and I ask pardon of all whom I have injured.

AN ACT OF CONTRITION

O my God, I am heartily sorry for having offended You, and I detest all my sins, because of Your just punishments, but most of all because they offend You, my God, who are all good and deserving of all my love. I firmly resolve, with the help of Your grace, to sin no more and to avoid the near occasions of sin.

HAIL, HOLY QUEEN

Hail, holy Queen, Mother of mercy, our life, our sweetness, and our hope, to you do we cry, poor banished children of Eve; to you do we send up our sighs, mourning and weeping in this valley of tears. Turn then, most gracious advocate, your eyes of mercy toward us; and after this our exile, show unto us the blessed fruit of your womb, Jesus. O clement, O loving, O sweet Virgin Mary.

SHORT ACTS OF FAITH, HOPE, LOVE AND SORROW*

Lord, I believe in You: increase my faith.

I trust in You: strengthen my trust.

I love You: let me love You more and more.

I am sorry for my sins: deepen my sorrow.

ANGEL OF GOD

Angel of God, my Guardian dear, to whom His love entrusts me here; ever this day be at my side, to light and guard, to rule and guide. Amen.

FOR THE SOULS IN PURGATORY

Eternal rest grant them, Lord. And let perpetual light shine on them. May they rest in peace. Amen.

GRACE BEFORE MEALS

Bless us, O Lord, and these Your gifts which we are about to receive from Your bounty, through Christ our Lord. Amen.

GRACE AFTER MEALS

We give You thanks for all Your benefits, O almighty God, who lives and reigns forever. Amen.

MORNING OFFERING

O Jesus, through the Immaculate heart of Mary, I offer You my prayers, works, joys and sufferings of this day, for all the intentions of Your Sacred Heart, in union with the Holy Sacrifice of the Mass throughout the world, in reparation for my sins, for the intentions of all our associates, and in particular for the intention recommended this month by the Holy Father.

*from the Universal Prayer.

Guidelines for Christian Living

THE TEN COMMANDMENTS OF GOD

1. I, the Lord, am your God. You shall not have other gods besides me.
2. You shall not take the name of the Lord, your God, in vain.
3. Remember to keep holy the Lord's day.
4. Honor your father and your mother.
5. You shall not kill.
6. You shall not commit adultery.
7. You shall not steal.
8. You shall not bear false witness against your neighbor.
9. You shall not covet your neighbor's wife.
10. You shall not covet anything that belongs to your neighbor.

THE TWO GREAT COMMANDMENTS

You shall love the Lord your God
with all your heart,
with all your soul,
with all your mind
and with all your strength.
You shall love your neighbor as yourself.

THE SEVEN SACRAMENTS

Baptism
Confirmation
Holy Eucharist
Penance
Anointing of the Sick
Holy Orders
Matrimony

THE THEOLOGICAL VIRTUES

Faith
Hope
Charity

THE CARDINAL VIRTUES

Prudence
Justice
Fortitude
Temperance

SPECIAL DUTIES OF CATHOLIC CHRISTIANS

1. To keep holy the day of the Lord's Resurrection: to worship God by participating in Mass every Sunday and holy day of obligation.* We are also to abstain from such work or business that would inhibit the worship given to God, the joy proper to the Lord's day, or due relaxation of mind and body.
2. To lead a sacramental life: to receive Holy Communion frequently and the Sacrament of Penance regularly
   —minimally, to receive the Sacrament of Penance at least once a year (annual confession is obligatory only if serious sin is involved).
   —minimally, to receive Holy Communion at least once a year. This precept must be fulfilled during Paschal time unless for a good reason it is fulfilled at another time of year.
3. To study Catholic teaching in preparation for the Sacrament of Confirmation, to be confirmed, and then to continue to study and advance the cause of Christ.
4. To observe the marriage laws of the Church: to give religious training (by example and word) to one's children; to use parish schools and religious education programs.
5. To strengthen and support the Church: one's own parish community and parish priests; the worldwide Church and the Holy Father.
6. To do penance, including abstaining from meat and fasting from food on the appointed days.
7. To join in the missionary spirit and apostolate of the Church.

THE GIFTS OF THE HOLY SPIRIT

Wisdom
Understanding
Right Judgment (Counsel)
Courage (Fortitude)
Knowledge
Love (Piety)
Reverence (Fear of the Lord)

THE EIGHT BEATITUDES

1. Blest are the poor in spirit: the reign of God is theirs.
2. Blest are the sorrowing: they shall be consoled.
3. Blest are the lowly: they shall inherit the land.
4. Blest are they who hunger and thirst for holiness: they shall have their fill.
5. Blest are they who show mercy: mercy shall be theirs.
6. Blest are the single-hearted: for they shall see God.
7. Blest are the peacemakers: they shall be called sons of God.
8. Blest are those persecuted for holiness' sake: the reign of God is theirs.

THE WORKS OF MERCY
Spiritual

1. To admonish the sinner.
2. To instruct the ignorant
3. To counsel the doubtful
4. To comfort the sorrowful
5. To bear wrongs patiently
6. To forgive all injuries
7. To pray for the living and the dead

Corporal

1. To feed the hungry
2. To give drink to the thirsty
3. To clothe the naked
4. To visit the imprisoned
5. To shelter the homeless
6. To visit the sick
7. To bury the dead

*In the United States, these days are: Christmas (December 25); Mary, Mother of God (January 1); Ascension Thursday; the Assumption (August 15); All Saints' Day (November 1); the Immaculate Conception (December 8).

Some Basic Truths of Our Faith

GOD AND OURSELVES

1. Who is God?
God is the Creator of heaven and earth, of all that is seen and unseen.

2. What does "Creator" mean?
A Creator is one who makes from nothing. The only Creator is God.

3. What is God like?
God is a pure spirit. He is completely perfect—all-knowing, all-good, all-powerful and all-loving.

4. What is the mystery of the Blessed Trinity?
The mystery of the Blessed Trinity is one God in three divine persons: the Father, the Son and the Holy Spirit.

5. Does God care about us?
God cares about us very much. He keeps us in existence, helps us in everything we do, and watches over us with love.

6. How do we know about God?
We know about God through what He has created and especially through the Catholic Church and the Bible.

7. What is the Bible?
The Bible is the Holy Book in which God speaks to us through the words of men who wrote what He wanted them to write.

8. What is the meaning of life?
God gave us life so that we will use it to know Him, love Him and serve Him now and be happy with Him forever in heaven.

9. How do we learn to know, love and serve God?
We learn to know, love and serve God from the teachings and examples of Jesus Christ.

10. Who is Jesus Christ?
Jesus Christ is God the Son, who became man for us while remaining God.

11. Where do we find the teachings and examples of Jesus Christ?
We find the teachings and examples of Jesus Christ in the Bible, especially in the four Gospels.

12. What is the Incarnation?
The Incarnation is the taking of a human nature by God the Son.

13. Why did God become man?
God became man to save us from our sins, give us His grace, and teach us what we must believe and do to reach heaven.

14. What is the Redemption?
The Redemption is Jesus' death and resurrection, by which He made up for our sins and won for us the help we need for reaching heaven.

15. What do we learn from Jesus' choice of death for our sake?
From Jesus' choice of death for our sake we learn how much He loves us and how terrible sin is.

SIN

16. What is sin?
Sin is disobedience to God and His laws.

17. What is original sin?
Original sin is the lack of grace with which each of us came into the world because of the sin of our first parents.

18. What is personal sin?
Personal sin is personal disobedience to God's law through a willful thought, desire, word, action or omission.

19. What does sin do to a person?
Serious (mortal) sin drives out God's grace. Lesser (venial) sin weakens the person's friendship with God.

GRACE

20. What is grace?
Grace is a gift that God gives us to bring us closer to Him.

21. What is sanctifying grace?
Sanctifying grace is a sharing in God's own life that makes us holy (close to Him).

22. What is actual grace?
Actual grace is light for our mind and strength for our will, which God gives us whenever we need it.

23. Why is grace important?
Grace is important because we need God's life and help in order to please Him in life and enter His happiness after death.

THE VIRGIN MARY

24. Who is Mary?
Mary is the Mother of Jesus and therefore the Mother of God.

25. Why do we call Mary our Mother?
We call Mary our Mother because Jesus Himself made her the spiritual Mother of the Church and of each one of us.

26. What is the Immaculate Conception?
The Immaculate Conception is Mary's freedom from original sin from the first moment of her existence.

27. What is the Assumption?
The Assumption is the taking up of the Blessed Virgin Mary into heaven body and soul by God's power.

THE CATHOLIC CHURCH

28. What is the Catholic Church?
The Catholic Church is God's people, whom He has joined together in the same beliefs, laws and sacraments under the Pope.

29. Why did Jesus Christ found the Church?
Jesus Christ founded the Church in order to continue His mission on earth—that is, to save mankind.

30. Who was St. Peter?
St. Peter was the apostle whom Jesus chose to be the first Pope.

31. Who is the Pope?
The Pope is Jesus' representative (vicar) on earth.

32. Is the Pope the head of the Church?
The Pope is the *visible* head of the Church and Jesus is its *invisible* Head.

33. Why did Jesus give us the Pope?
Jesus gave us the Pope for the sake of the unity of the Church.

34. Who are the bishops?
The bishops are the leaders of the Church, united with the Pope and under him.

35. What does Jesus do for us through the Church?
Through the Church Jesus gives us grace and teaches us what we must believe and do in order to reach heaven.

36. What is infallibility?
Infallibility is God-given freedom from making mistakes in matters of faith and morals, which belongs under certain conditions to the Pope and the bishops united with him.

37. Why is infallibility important?
Infallibility is important because it guarantees to the Catholic Church the sureness of God's truth.

38. Why is it important to live a real Catholic life?
It is important to live a real Catholic life because the Catholic Church has the sureness of Christ's truth and the fullness of His grace.

THE SACRAMENTS

39. How does the life of grace come to us?
The life of grace comes to us chiefly through the Mass and the other sacraments.

40. What is the Mass?
The Mass is the sacrifice of the cross taking place today; a memorial of Jesus' death and resurrection; a holy meal in which we receive Christ Himself.

41. What are the sacraments?
The sacraments are seven special actions of Jesus through which He gives us His Spirit to make us holy by grace.

42. What are the names of the seven sacraments?
The seven sacraments are: Baptism, Confirmation, Holy Eucharist, Penance, Anointing of the Sick, Holy Orders and Matrimony.

43. What is Baptism?
Baptism is the sacrament in which Jesus sends us His Spirit to free us from sin, seal us as Christians, and give us His grace.

44. What did the grace of Baptism do for us?

The grace of Baptism made us God's children, heirs of heaven, living members of the Church and temples of the Blessed Trinity, the Father, the Son and the Holy Spirit.

45. What is Confirmation?

Confirmation is the sacrament in which the Holy Spirit joins us more closely to Jesus and His Church, strengthens our faith, and seals us as Christ's witnesses.

46. What is the Eucharist?

The Eucharist is the sacrament of Jesus' real and complete presence, in which He renews His sacrifice, comes to us as Holy Communion, and remains close to us in our churches.

47. What is Penance?

Penance is the sacrament in which Jesus forgives our sins, strengthens or renews our friendship with Himself and His people, and gives us the strength to do better.

48. How do we receive the sacrament of Penance?

To receive the sacrament of Penance we: remember our sins; are sorry for them; intend not to commit them again; tell them in confession; say or do our penance.

49. What are mortal and venial sins?

Mortal sins are serious disobediences to God and His law, which must be told in confession. Venial sins are less serious disobediences.

50. When is a sin mortal?

A sin is mortal when the person knew before or while committing it that it was seriously wrong, yet freely and deliberately decided to do it.

51. What is the Anointing of the Sick?

The Anointing of the Sick is the sacrament in which Jesus brings healing of soul and often of body to sick or injured people in danger of death.

52. What is Holy Orders?

Holy Orders is the sacrament through which Jesus gives His Spirit to men to seal them as deacons, priests and bishops and to give them the powers that belong to each position.

53. What is Matrimony?

Matrimony is the sacrament through which Jesus blesses a marriage and gives the couple the grace to love one another faithfully throughout life, to love their children and to raise their children as good Christians.

54. Why are the sacraments important?

The sacraments are important because they are the chief ways in which we receive or grow in God's grace and are strengthened to live as we should.

THE COMMANDMENTS OF GOD

55. What are God's ten commandments?

God's ten commandments are laws which guide us in living the way all human beings should live.

56. What does God tell us in the first commandment?

In the first commandment God tells us that we should pray to Him, believe His teachings, trust Him and love Him.

57. What are some of the sins forbidden by the first commandment?

Some of the sins forbidden by the first commandment are: giving up the Catholic religion; refusing to believe one or more of the Church's teachings; reading books or pamphlets against the Catholic faith; practicing superstition.

58. What does God tell us in the second commandment?

In the second commandment God tells us to speak with respect of Him, of holy things, of holy places and of persons close to Him.

59. What are some of the sins forbidden by the second commandment?

Some of the sins forbidden by the second commandment are: using the names of God or Jesus in a wrong way; insulting God or religion; perjury (lying when under oath).

60. What does God tell us in the third commandment?

In the third commandment God tells us to make Sunday special by worshiping Him at Mass (which may also be done on Saturday evening) and by taking the rest we need.

61. What are some of the sins forbidden by the third commandment?

Some of the sins forbidden by the third commandment are: missing Mass on Sunday (Saturday evening); being late for Mass on purpose; doing unnecessary hard work on Sunday.

62. What does God tell us in the fourth commandment?

In the fourth commandment God tells us to love, respect, obey and help our parents and to respect and obey others who are in charge of us, such as teachers, the leaders of our Church and country, etc.

63. What are some of the sins forbidden by the fourth commandment?

Some of the sins forbidden by the fourth commandment are: disobeying one's parents; hating, striking or insulting them; speaking or acting unkindly toward them; causing them anger or sorrow.

64. What does God tell us in the fifth commandment?

In the fifth commandment God tells us to look after the life, health, safety and spiritual good of ourselves and others.

65. What are some of the sins forbidden by the fifth commandment?

Some of the sins forbidden by the fifth commandment are: murder; abortion; suicide; euthanasia (mercy killing); drunkenness; drug taking; unnecessary risk of life; anger; hatred; fighting; leading others to sin.

66. What does God tell us in the sixth and ninth commandments?

In the sixth and ninth commandments God tells us to respect His gift of sex by avoiding the thoughts, desires and actions that are permitted only to married people, and by avoiding conversations, ways of dressing, pictures, books, etc., which could lead us or others to sin.

67. What are some of the sins forbidden by the sixth and ninth commandments?

Some of the sins forbidden by the sixth and ninth commandments are: adultery[1], fornication[2], contraception[3], homosexuality, masturbation, deliberate thoughts, words or actions that arouse sexual feelings.

68. How can we help ourselves to keep the sixth and ninth commandments?

We can help ourselves to keep the sixth and ninth commandments by praying often, especially to the Virgin Mary; by receiving Penance and the Eucharist often; by keeping ourselves busy; and by avoiding persons, places or things that might tempt us to sin.

69. What does God tell us in the seventh and tenth commandments?

In the seventh and tenth commandments God tells us to take care of our own things, to respect what belongs to others and to make up for any stealing or harming of property that we have done deliberately.

70. What are some of the sins forbidden by the seventh and tenth commandments?

Some of the sins forbidden by the seventh and tenth commandments are: stealing; wanting to steal; unjustly keeping what is not ours; cheating; willfully damaging the property of others; wasting time or materials when working; not paying what we owe.

71. What does God tell us in the eighth commandment?

In the eighth commandment God tells us to say only what is true and good, and if we have injured someone's reputation to make up for the harm we have done.

72. What are some of the sins forbidden by the eighth commandment?

Some of the sins forbidden by the eighth commandment are: lying; insulting; harming someone's reputation; criticizing unfairly; not keeping secrets that we should keep.

---

1. Sexual relations between two persons, one of whom is married to someone else.

2. Sexual relations between unmarried persons.

3. Artificial birth control.

JESUS, CENTER OF HISTORY

OLD

creation and fall (sin) of man
promise of salvation
covenant with Abraham
(about 19th century B.C.)
Exodus and Sinai covenant
(about 13th century B.C.)
conquest and kingdoms
(12th–7th centuries B.C.)
exile and restoration
(6th century B.C.)
persecution and liberation
(2nd century B.C.)
era of expectancy
(1st century B.C.)

COVENANT

JESUS CHRIST, CENTER OF HISTORY

incarnation, life, teachings, passion, death,   resurrection, ascension, sending of the Spirit

apostolic age
(1st century A.D.)
age of persecutions
(1st–4th centuries A.D.)
barbarian invasions
(4th–6th centuries A.D.)
cultural recovery
(6th–13th centuries A.D.)
disagreements and reforms
(14th–16th centuries A.D.)
missionary expansion
(16th–20th centuries A.D.)
struggle against secularism
(now)

NEW   **COVENANT**

resurrection of the dead
universal judgment
eternity of heaven and of hell

THE BOOKS OF THE BIBLE

OLD TESTAMENT

HISTORICAL BOOKS (God speaks through history and stories): Genesis, Exodus, Leviticus, Numbers, Deuteronomy, Joshua, Judges, Ruth, 1 Samuel, 2 Samuel, 1 Kings, 2 Kings, 1 Chronicles, 2 Chronicles, Ezra, Nehemiah, Tobit, Judith, Esther, 1 Maccabees, 2 Maccabees

WISDOM BOOKS (God speaks through prayers and holy teachings): Job, Psalms, Proverbs, Ecclesiastes, Song of Songs, Wisdom, Sirach

PROPHETIC BOOKS (God speaks through what His prophets—messengers—said and did): Isaiah, Jeremiah, Lamentations, Baruch, Ezekiel, Daniel, Hosea, Joel, Amos, Obadiah, Jonah, Micah, Nahum, Habakkuk, Zephaniah, Haggai, Zechariah, Malachi

NEW TESTAMENT

HISTORICAL BOOKS (God speaks through His Son and the history of the early Church): Matthew, Mark, Luke, John, Acts of the Apostles

INSTRUCTIONAL BOOKS (God speaks through the letters of the first Christians): Romans, 1 Corinthians, 2 Corinthians, Galatians, Ephesians, Philippians, Colossians, 1 Thessalonians, 2 Thessalonians, 1 Timothy, 2 Timothy, Titus, Philemon, Hebrews; James, 1 Peter, 2 Peter, 1 John, 2 John, 3 John, Jude

APOCALYPTIC BOOK (God speaks through an account of visions written to encourage the persecuted people of God): Revelation

THE TWELVE APOSTLES AND THEIR FEAST DAYS

Simon Peter—June 29; Andrew—November 30; James, son of Zebedee—July 25; John—December 27; Philip—May 3; Bartholomew (Nathanael)—August 24; Matthew (Levi)—September 21; Thomas—July 3; James, son of Alphaeus—May 3; Simon the Zealot—October 28; Jude (Thaddeus)—October 28; Matthias—May 14

Peter and Andrew were brothers. So were James and John, the sons of Zebedee. After Jesus' ascension, Matthias was chosen to replace Judas Iscariot, who had become a traitor.

HOW TO GAIN INDULGENCES

An indulgence is the removal of temporal punishment of forgiven sins. We are able to gain indulgences because Jesus gave His Church the power to let us share in the merits of Jesus, Mary and the saints.

A **plenary** indulgence takes away **all** the temporal punishment for remitted sins that we would have had to suffer on earth or in purgatory. If we go to confession and Communion within a few days (before or after), pray for the Pope (for example, one Our Father and Hail Mary), and are free from any attachment to sin, we can gain a plenary indulgence for:
- visiting our Savior in the Blessed Sacrament for at least half an hour
- or reading the Bible for half an hour
- or making the stations of the cross with devotion
- or performing certain other good actions suggested by the Church.

It is recommended that the required Communion be received on the same day that the indulgenced good work is done.

A **partial** indulgence takes away **some** of the temporal punishment for sins that we would have had to suffer. We can receive a partial indulgence for praying with trust while we patiently put up with the difficulties of life and do our work as well as we can, or for performing works of mercy, or for making sacrifices and offering them up to God. There are many other ways we can gain a partial indulgence.

Many people gain indulgences for the souls in purgatory rather than for themselves. This is great love for the faithful departed. At the same time it is great gain for us too, because while the souls in purgatory cannot pray for themselves it is generally believed that they can pray for us.

Glossary

A

abortion—the deliberate destruction of an unborn child.

absolution—the freeing of a person from his or her sins by Jesus through the priest who hears confession.

abstinence—refraining from eating meat, and soups and gravies made from meat, on certain "days of abstinence," such as Ash Wednesday.

act of contrition—a prayer of sorrow for offending God, who is so good.

acts of faith, hope, love—prayers that express our belief, our trust, and our love for God.

actual graces—temporary helps from the Holy Spirit which make us able to know and do what God expects of us at a certain moment.

actual sin—see personal sin.

admonish—to warn.

adore—praise and worship God.

adultery—the sin of sexual intercourse between a married person and someone who is not his or her married partner.

Advent—"coming"; the season in which we prepare for Christmas and recall Christ's second coming at the end of time.

All Saints Day—a holy day of obligation celebrated once a year in honor of all the saints.

alleluia—a Hebrew word—now used in Christian worship—which means "praise God" or "may God be praised."

altar cloth (Mass)—a piece of material usually made from cotton fibers which covers the altar.

amen—a Hebrew word meaning "yes" or "certainly," used by Christians to conclude prayers and express faith in the Eucharist when receiving Communion.

angels—spirits without bodies, created by God.

Angelus—a special prayer that honors the Incarnation of the Son of God said morning, noon and evening.

anger—strong displeasure; wrath; one of the capital sins.

Annunciation—the day (celebrated March 25) on which the Church recalls the Angel Gabriel's announcement to Mary, her acceptance, and the Incarnation of the Son of God.

Anointing of the Sick—the sacrament by which Christ gives comfort and strength to the soul, and sometimes to the body, of someone who is dangerously ill due to sickness, injury, or old age.

Apostles—"those who are sent"—the men chosen by Jesus to be the first leaders (bishops) of His Church.

apostolate—the work of living and sharing the Catholic Faith so that people may be brought to God.

apostolic—connected with the apostles.

archbishop—the bishop of an important diocese (archdiocese), who has a certain amount of authority over the bishops of neighboring dioceses.

archdiocese—the diocese governed by an archbishop.

artificial birth control—the practice, condemned by the Church, by which pills, drugs or mechanical devices are used to stop the transmission of human life.

Ascension—Jesus' visible departure from this earth; the Thursday on which we remember this event (a holy day of obligation 40 days after Easter).

ashes (blessed)—burned palm branches traced on our forehead in the form of a cross on Ash Wednesday to remind us of our death.

aspiration—a very short prayer, such as: "My Jesus, mercy!"

Assumption—the taking up of the Blessed Virgin into heaven body and soul by God's power; the holy day of obligation (August 15) on which we celebrate the memory of this event.

atheist—a person who claims that there is no God, or at least lives as if there were none.

atone—to make up for sin.

autonomous—independent; self-governing.

B

Baptism—the sacrament in which Jesus sends us His Spirit, who frees us from sin and gives us the grace by which we become God's children, heirs of heaven, members of the Church, temples of the Blessed Trinity.

baptism of blood—the reception of grace by an unbaptized person because he or she gives his life for love of Christ or a Christian virtue.

baptism of desire—the reception of grace because of perfect love of God or perfect contrition for sin and the desire to do His will. In other words, if the person knew of Baptism and was able to receive it, he would be baptized.

Beatific Vision—the clear and immediate knowledge of God enjoyed by the angels and saints in heaven.

beatification—the Church's official declaration that a person is in heaven—a step on the way to canonization (declaration of sainthood).

beatitudes—promises of happiness as a reward for following Jesus in a more perfect way.

being—the quality of existence of a living thing (usually refers to human persons).

Benediction—see Eucharistic Benediction.

Bible—see Scripture.

bishops—leaders of the Church who hold the place of the Apostles.

blessed—the souls of the dead who are in heaven; the title given to a person who has been beatified.

Blessed Sacrament—another name for the Holy Eucharist.

Blessed Trinity—(see Trinity).

Blessed Virgin Mary—the Mother of Jesus and therefore the Mother of God.

blessings—words and actions by which a thing or a person is placed under the care of God.

Body of Christ—the Eucharist.

body of Christ—Christ's followers, joined together by the Holy Spirit and grace.

bribe—an offering of money or other valuable objects with the intention to corrupt.

C

calumny—the sin of harming another's good name through lies.

Canaan—one of the earlier names for the land of Palestine—Jesus' homeland.

canonized—declared a saint officially by the Church.

capital sins—seven inclinations or tendencies toward sin.

cardinal—a bishop (or priest) whom the Pope has chosen to belong to a special group of his advisors (and to elect a new Pope when the time comes).

cardinal virtues—four "key" or "hinge" virtues on which all the other virtues about right living (moral virtues) depend—these four are: prudence, justice, fortitude and temperance.

virtues—habits of doing good; habits that are holy (some examples are obedience, patience, charity...).

Catholic—a member of the Catholic Church, which is distinguished from all other Christian Churches by its loyalty to the Pope.

catholic (or universal)—the Church's characteristic of being for all people.

Catholic Church—the true Church founded by Jesus Christ, which can be known by these characteristics together: loyalty to the Pope and the bishops joined with him, oneness in belief, the sacrifice of the Mass, and the seven sacraments.

Catholic faith—the teachings of the Catholic Church; what we believe.

catholicity—universality; the Church's characteristic of being for all men.

character—a lasting spiritual seal or mark that expresses consecration.

charity—a power by which we love God above everything and we love all other people for His sake.

chastity—the virtue of those who keep the sixth and ninth commandments; also, the name of one of the vows made by religious, which involves giving up marriage and family life.

chemical dependency—addicted to alcohol or drugs.

Chosen People—The Jewish People of the Old Testament, who were chosen to be close to God in a special way; Christians, who are even more privileged.

chrism—a blessed mixture of oil and some aromatic substance used during the baptismal ceremony, in confirmation, during the ordination of priests and bishops, and in the consecration of churches, altars, etc.

Christian—a baptized follower of Jesus Christ.

Christian morality—living in a way worthy of our dignity as human beings and God's adopted children.

Christmas—the holy day of obligation on which we celebrate Jesus' birth.

Church—a word meaning gathering or community, used as the name of all Jesus' baptized followers united in the same faith, sacrifice and sacraments under the Pope and the bishops united with him (the Church on earth may be called the pilgrim Church; the souls in purgatory, the suffering Church; the Church in heaven, the blessed Church or Church of the blessed).

civil—relating to the state.

clergy—men who are ordained ministers of the Church (deacons, priests, bishops).

commandments—see Ten Commandments.

Communion—the receiving of Jesus in the Holy Eucharist.

communion of saints—the communication of spiritual help among God's faithful people on earth, in purgatory and in heaven.

community life—an essential factor in religious life. It consists of the religious community's serene living together, sharing the same life of prayer, labor, the same food, accommodations, and schedule, united in a common ideal.

compassion—deep sympathy; sorrow or pity for one who is suffering.

concelebration—the offering of Mass by two or more priests together.

conception—beginning of human life in the womb.

confidentiality—communication done in secret.

confirm—strengthen. In Confirmation our faith is deepened and strengthened. We are more perfectly bound to Christ and His Church.

Confirmation—the sacrament in which the Holy Spirit comes to us in a special way to join us more closely to Jesus and His Church.

conscience—a personal judgment (decision) that something is right or wrong because of the law and will of God.

Consecration (Mass)—the most important moment of the Mass, in which Jesus changes bread and wine into His Body and Blood as the priest says: "This is my body. This is the cup of my blood."

contraception—prevention of the beginning of a new human life.

contrition—sorrow for sin because it offends God.

conversion—a changing of one's way of life for the better.

convert—popular term for an adult who becomes a Catholic.

corporal (Mass)—a piece of linen on which rests the vessels holding the sacred species during Mass.

corporal works of mercy—to feed the hungry, to give drink to the thirsty, to clothe the naked, to shelter the homeless, to visit the sick, to visit the imprisoned, to bury the dead.

covenant—a lasting alliance or agreement of friendship.

covet—to want to take.

covetousness—a poorly controlled (or uncontrolled) desire for things one does not have; greed.

create—bring something out of nothing, which only God can do.

creature—anyone and anything created by God.

creed—a prayer in which we declare what we believe—for example, the Apostles' Creed or the Creed of the Mass (Nicene Creed).

crucifix—a cross on which the image of Jesus is represented.

crucifixion—death on a cross.

D

deacons—ordained ministers who help priests by baptizing, reading God's Word to the faithful, preaching, distributing Communion, giving Eucharistic Benediction, blessing couples who receive the sacrament of Matrimony, and performing many works of service.

death—the separation of soul and body, when the body becomes lifeless while the soul continues to live.

Deposit of Faith—divine revelation as contained in Sacred Scripture and Sacred Tradition.

detraction—the sin of making a person's hidden faults known without a good reason.

devil—any of the angels who turned against God and now tempt human beings to turn against Him.

diocese—a territory made up of parishes placed by the Pope under the care of a Church leader called an "ordinary."

disciple—a "pupil."

discrimination—unfairness to certain people or groups because of race, nationality, color, religion or similar reasons.

divine—referring to God.

divine providence—God's loving, fatherly care for His creatures.

divorce—in the eyes of law courts, the breaking of a marriage; in the eyes of God and the Church, a separation with no possibility of remarrying.

Doctor of the Church—a title given by the Church to certain learned and holy persons of the past.

dogma—a doctrine formally stated and authoritatively proclaimed to all Catholics by the Church.

E

Easter—the Church's greatest day of celebration—on which we rejoice over Jesus' resurrection.

Easter duty—the duty of receiving Holy Communion at least once a year—between the first Sunday of Lent and the Sunday after Pentecost (Trinity Sunday). For a good reason the precept may be fulfilled at another time during the year.

ecclesiastical—relating to the Church as a formal, established institution.

ecumenical council—a meeting of the bishops of the whole world called together by the Pope to discuss and explain Church teaching and to set forth guidelines for the People of God (a council's conclusions have value only if approved by the Pope).

energy—capacity for acting or working.

envy—the capital sin of sadness at another's success.

epistle—a letter written by one of the apostles which has become a book of the New Testament.

eternal—without beginning or end.

Eucharist—the sacrament of Jesus' complete presence, in which (under the appearances of bread and wine) He offers His sacrifice again, comes to His people as their spiritual food, and remains in our midst to be close to us and help us.

Eucharistic Benediction—the ceremony in which the priest blesses the people with the consecrated host enclosed in a sacred vessel called a monstrance which is visible to the worshiping community.

219

Eucharistic Celebration—another name for the Mass.

Eucharistic Congress—a gathering of Catholics to honor the Blessed Sacrament through Masses, Benedictions, processions, sermons, etc.

euthanasia—a form of murder or suicide in which a person's life is taken with the excuse of avoiding pain, shortening sufferings, etc.

evangelical counsels—a term meaning "advice given in the Gospels," used when speaking of the poverty, chastity and obedience that religious freely choose in order to grow closer to Christ.

evangelists—the four Gospel writers.

evangelization—spreading the Good News (the Gospel message).

evolution—the theory of development through change, often used in reference to the development of plants, animals and human beings (their bodies only. Each human soul is directly created by God.)

ex cathedra—a Latin term which means "from the chair" of St. Peter. It is used when referring to the Pope's infallible statements regarding what Catholics must believe and live.

examination of conscience—reflection for the purpose of discovering or recalling sins committed.

Exile—the period of the chosen people's captivity in Babylon.

Exodus—the journey of the Israelites from slavery in Egypt.

exorcism—the driving out of evil spirits by a priest through the power of God.

F

faith—a God-given power and habit by which we believe in Him and everything He has taught us.

Faith—what we believe; our Catholic religion.

faithful—loyal followers of the Lord Jesus; the baptized who have declared their faith as members of the Catholic Church.

fast—eating less in order to do penance, grow in self-control, progress in love of God, etc.

Fathers of the Church—Christian writers of the early centuries who had some connection with the apostles, as well as the holy and wise Christian writers through the eighth century.

First Five Saturdays—the custom of assisting at the Eucharistic Celebration and receiving Holy Communion for five consecutive first Saturday's in honor of Our Lady. We ask her for the grace to live and die well.

five senses—sight, hearing, touch, taste and smell.

fornication—the sin of sexual intercourse between unmarried persons.

fortitude—the cardinal virtue by which a person does what is good and right in spite of any difficulty.

fruits of the Holy Spirit—good deeds and habits that result from our response to the Holy Spirit's impulses to do good (actual graces). The fruits are: charity, joy, peace, patience, kindness, goodness, long-suffering, humility, fidelity, modesty, continence, chastity.

G

Gifts of the Holy Spirit—seven special helps from the Holy Spirit that keep us ready to recognize and welcome His actual graces. Their names are wisdom, understanding, right judgment (or counsel), courage (or fortitude), knowledge, love (or piety) and reverence (or fear of the Lord).

glory—the splendor of God in heaven; the happiness of the angels and saints in heaven; the praise given to God by His creatures.

gluttony—the capital sin that inclines a person toward too much eating and drinking.

God the Father—the first Person of the Trinity, who watches over us with the love of a father.

God the Holy Spirit—the third Person of the Trinity, sent by the Father and the Son to live in us and in the Church; the Spirit of truth and love.

God the Son—the second Person of the Trinity, who became man, died and rose to save us; He is the God-man, Jesus Christ.

godparent—the godfather and godmother who are sponsors at Baptism. They are responsible for the child's religious training if the parents neglect their duty or die.

good will—right intention; to act for and with sincere motives.

H

heaven—everlasting life and happiness with God.

Hebrews—the people descended from Abraham, whom God chose to prepare the world for the coming of the Savior (also called *Israelites* around the time of the Exodus and *Jewish people* after the Exile); also the title of a New Testament epistle.

heir—a person who will receive something that belongs to his or her family.

hell—everlasting suffering and separation from God.

heresy—the deliberate denial of a truth of faith.

hermit—one who lives in solitude especially for religious reasons.

hierarchy—the Church's teaching authority, especially the Pope and bishops, but also priests and deacons.

holiness—closeness to God through grace, love, goodness, separation from sin.

holy—belonging to God; close to God; "like God"; Christ-like; also a mark of the Church.

holy days of obligation—certain days besides Sundays on which Catholic Christians are expected to take part in the Mass (in the United States they are: Christmas (December 25), Solemnity of the Mother of God (January 1), Ascension Thursday, the Assumption (August 15), All Saints' Day (November 1), the Immaculate Conception (December 8).

Holy Eucharist—see Eucharist.

Holy Family—Jesus, Mary and Joseph.

Holy Father—another name for the Pope.

Holy Land—Palestine, the homeland of Jesus.

Holy Orders—the sacrament through which Jesus gives His Spirit to men to make them deacons, priests and bishops and gives them the powers that belong to each status.

Holy See—the diocese of the Pope, also the center of the Church's government, located at Rome (Vatican City), from which the Pope and all those who help him see to the needs of the worldwide Church.

Holy Thursday—the Thursday before Easter, on which we especially remember Jesus' gift of the Eucharist.

holy water—water blessed by a priest in order to give God's blessing to those who use it.

Holy Year—a year in which a special "jubilee" indulgence may be received; a year of special pilgrimages to Rome.

homosexual activity—impure relations with someone of the same sex (seriously sinful).

hope—the power and habit of trusting that our all-powerful and faithful God will bring us to eternal happiness if we do our part.

hosanna—a shout of joy taken from the Psalms which means, "Do save us!"

human—that which pertains to people.

humility—the virtue by which we truly know ourselves and see that whatever is good in us comes from God.

hypocrisy—pretending to appear as something one is not.

Hypostatic Union—the union of the human and divine natures in the one divine Person of Christ.

I

Immaculate Conception—freedom from original sin from the very moment of conception—a privilege that God gave to the Blessed Mother; the holy day of obligation (December 8) on which this event is honored.

immodesty—lack of decency in dress or way of acting.

immortal—undying.

impeccability—incapable of sinning (not to be confused with infallibility).

imperfect contrition—sorrow for sin for reasons that are good but not the very best—for example, for out of fear than out of love.

imperishable—a characteristic of the Church whereby she cannot be destroyed.

impure thoughts—immoral imaginnings or considerations which become sinful if we freely consent to allow them to remain.

impurity—any sexual pleasure (in thoughts, desires or actions) forbidden by the sixth and ninth commandments.

Incarnation—the taking of a human body and soul (human nature) by God the Son.

indefectible—the Church's characteristic of being faithful to Christ until the end of time because He is with it as He promised (see Matthew 28:20).

indissolubility—"unbreakableness"; a characteristic of marriage by which it lasts until the death of husband or wife.

individual judgment—the judgment of a person by Christ immediately after death.

indulgence—the removal of some or all of the temporal punishment for sin that we should have had to suffer on earth or in purgatory.

infallibility—freedom from making a mistake when teaching a truth of faith or right living (a gift given by the Holy Spirit in certain circumstances to the Pope and the bishops united with him).

infinite—perfect, without limitation.

inspiration—the special guidance that the Holy Spirit gave to the Bible's human authors, so that they wrote everything God wanted them to write and only that.

inspirations—temporary helps from the Holy Spirit which make us able to know and do what God expects of us at a certain moment; actual graces.

intercede—to pray for someone else.

Israelites—the name by which Abraham's descendants, the Jewish people, were called around the time of the Exodus.

J

Jesus—"Savior"—the name taken by the second Person of the Trinity after He became man.

Judaism—the religion of the Old Testament, still followed today by the Jewish people.

jurisdiction—the power or authority of administering law or justice.

justice—fairness; giving everyone what he or she deserves.

K

kingdom of heaven—both the kingdom of God in this world (the Church) and that of the next world (heaven).

L

laity—the faithful who are not clerics or ordained religious.

Last Supper—The Passover Feast celebrated by Jesus and His Apostles at which He gave us the Eucharist.

Lent—the Church's season of preparation for Easter in which Christians are expected to give more attention to prayer, penance and good deeds.

lie—something said usually for the purpose of deceiving others, which we know or suspect to be untrue.

Liturgical Year—the Church's year, composed of special seasons for thinking and prayer about certain mysteries of our Faith so that they will affect our lives and help us live as better Christians.

liturgy—all the ceremonies that the Church uses for worship as a community (public worship).

Lord's Day—in the Old Testament and for the present-day Jewish people, Saturday; for Christians, Sunday.

lowly—aware of one's limitations and faults; humble.

lust—the capital sin of uncontrolled sexual desire.

M

magisterium—the Church's teaching authority (the Pope and the bishops united with him).

manna—food which was provided by God for the Israelites during their journey from Egypt.

marks of the Church—four characteristics of Jesus' Church by which the same Church may be recognized today: unity or oneness, holiness, catholicity or universality and apostolicity.

martyr—a person who allows himself or herself to be put to death because of the Christian Faith.

Mass—the very sacrifice of the cross taking place today on our altars; a memorial of Jesus' death, resurrection and ascension; a holy covenant meal in which we receive Jesus Himself.

Master—a title meaning "teacher" by which the Apostles called Jesus.

masturbation—self-abuse (seriously sinful).

Matrimony—the sacrament through which Jesus blesses a marriage, giving the couple the right to call upon Him for help in loving and being loyal to one another for life and in raising the children God will send them.

matter—that which is material.

Memorare—a prayer to our Blessed Mother composed by Saint Bernard.

memorial—the recalling of a past event.

mercy—forgiveness; loving help in time of need.

mercy-killing—through false pity, causing the termination of the life of one who is terminally ill.

merit—the "right" to a reward in heaven earned by those who have God's grace and pray or do good works for love of Him.

Messiah—the hoped for leader or savior of the Hebrew people; Jesus Christ, the Savior of all people.

mind—our reason or power to think.

miracle—an event that takes place outside of the ordinary working of nature's laws—something only God could do because He made the laws.

mission—a purpose, which for Christ and the Christian is the saving of the world; a Christian community established to give non-Christian peoples a chance to learn about Jesus and salvation.

missionaries—people dedicated to spreading God's Word (evangelizing), especially in mission countries.

mixed marriage—a marriage between a Catholic and a non-Catholic, for which the Catholic needs special Church permission, called a dispensation.

modesty—the avoidance of ways of dressing, acting, etc., that could lead oneself or others to sin against the sixth or ninth commandment.

monk—a member of a religious community of men who live a life of prayer and penance apart from the world.

monsignor—a title of honor given to some priests.

monstrance—a tall vessel in which the Blessed Sacrament may be placed for adoration (also called an ostensorium. Both words have the meaning of "showing").

moral—that which concerns right and wrong.

morality—living in a way worthy of our dignity as human beings.

mortal sin—a serious offense against God which drives grace out of the soul.

mystery—a great truth made known by God which our limited minds will never be able to fully understand.

mystical body—the real but unseen union of members of the Church (living and dead) with Jesus and one another, through the grace-giving activity of the Holy Spirit.

N

natural family planning—natural methods of birth control (as opposed to artificial), which the Church recognizes because these do not directly block God's creative action.

nature—essential quality or composition.

New Testament—the second part of the Bible, which tells about the life and teachings of Jesus and the life of the early Church.

O

oath—a declaration before God that what we say is true.

obligation—a moral duty.

occasions of sin—persons, places, or things that may make sin easy for us.

Old Testament—the first part of the Bible, which tells about the preparation of the Chosen People for the coming of the Savior, Jesus Christ.

omission—the failure to do something one should have done.

one—a mark of the Church which indicates that Jesus' Church is united in belief, worship and government.

Ordinary Time—the season of the Church year outside of the Advent-Christmas and Lent-Easter seasons—one part between the Christmas season and Lent; the other between Pentecost and Advent.

ordination—the ceremony in which a man is ordained a deacon, priest or bishop; receiving the sacrament of Holy Orders.

original sin—the lack of grace with which each of us comes into the world, because our first parents lost grace both for themselves and for us.

Orthodox—non-Catholic Christians who separated from the Catholic Church in the late Middle Ages. They have the Mass and the seven sacraments but do not accept the Pope as their chief leader.

P

Palestine—one of the names for Jesus' homeland.

papal—a word that refers to the Pope.

parable—a story that teaches a truth of religion or a principle of right living.

Paraclete—a name given to the Holy Spirit—meaning "one who pleads for our needs" (see Romans 8:26-27).

parish—a community of Christians who worship together in the same church and are led by the same priest, usually called a pastor.

parish priest—a priest who leads a community of Christians who worship together in the same church.

parochial—a word that refers to a parish.

partial indulgence—the shortening or lessening of some of the temporal punishment due to forgiven sin.

particular judgment—the judgment of a person by Christ immediately after death; individual judgment.

paschal—referring to either the Jewish Passover or the Christian Easter.

paschal mystery—The passion, death, resurrection and ascension of Jesus. "Paschal" is a word that refers to Passover and Easter; "mystery" here means event.

passion—the sufferings of Jesus before His death.

passions—feelings or drives such as desire or fear.

Passover—the Jewish feast held yearly in memory of the Exodus to freedom in the Sinai Peninsula.

Passover celebration—the Jewish feast held yearly in memory of the Exodus.

pastor—the chief priest or "shepherd" of a parish.

patron saint—a special saint to imitate and pray to; a heavenly protector, usually one's name saint.

Penance—(see: *Reconciliation*.)

penance—prayers or good works to make up for sin.

Pentecost—the Sunday seven weeks after Easter on which we celebrate the memory of the Holy Spirit's descent upon the Apostles.

People of God—the Church; the chosen people of the new covenant.

perfect contrition—sorrow for sin especially because sin displeases God, who is all-good and loving and deserves all our love.

perfection—the condition of being perfect—completely holy—toward which all Christians are called to work.

perjury—telling a lie after promising before God to tell only the truth.

perpetuate—to continue.

persecution—suffering caused by others because they are against what a person stands for.

person—a being with an intellect and free will; an individual.

personal sin—sin that we ourselves commit; actual sin (mortal or venial).

pilgrim—traveler on a holy journey.

pilgrimage—journey to a holy place for a holy purpose.

plenary indulgence—the removal of *all* the punishment a person would have had to suffer either in this life or in purgatory for remitted sin.

Pope—the chief teacher and leader of the Catholic Church; St. Peter's successor; the one who holds the place of Jesus in the Church.

pornography—writings, pictures, etc., calculated to stir up thoughts, desires and actions against the sixth and ninth commandments.

poverty—the condition of being poor; the name of a promise (vow) made by religious so their "treasure" will be in heaven.

prayer—talking with God with mind and heart and often with voice as well.

pre-marital sex—marriage (sex) relations carried out before marriage and therefore seriously sinful.

Precepts of the Church—special laws made by the Church for our spiritual good as Catholics; also called *duties of Catholic Christians*.

prejudice—strong biased opinion.

pride—too high an opinion of oneself; one of the seven capital sins.

priest—one who offers sacrifice; a man who has received from God, through Holy Orders, the power to offer Mass.

Prince of the Apostles—a title given to Saint Peter, the first Pope.

pro-life—having the conviction that all human life is precious because every human bieng is made in the image and likeness of God.

proclaim—to announce.

procurator—an agent of the Roman Empire who was in charge of a Roman Province (Pontius Pilate, for example, was procurator of Judea at the time of Jesus' death).

profess—to declare.

prophecy—may be concerned with future events, but it is basically the mediation and interpretation of the divine mind and will.

prophets—people who spoke for God or interpreted His message.

Protestants—non-Catholic Christians other than the Eastern Orthodox (there are hundreds of groups, called denominations).

providence—the loving care of God for His creatures, especially human beings; His way of "making things work together for the good" (cf. Romans 8:28). See also: *Divine Providence*.

prudence—the virtue by which a person puts heaven before everything else, thinks carefully before acting, makes wise choices, and does things well.

Public Life—the time on earth that Jesus spent preaching.

purgatory—a condition of suffering after death in which souls make up for their sins before they enter Heaven.

purity—the virtue by which we avoid immoral thoughts, words and actions and cultivate the opposite.

R

Rabbi—a Jewish religious leader.

racism—attitudes or actions that put down people of a certain race or races.

ransom—to obtain a person's release from captivity or slavery by paying for it.

rash judgment—the sin of thinking that a person has committed a sin when there is not enough evidence for such a conclusion.

Real Presence—the complete presence of Jesus in the Holy Eucharist as God and man.

reason—the power to think.

Reconciliation—the sacrament of God's loving forgiveness by which we are set free from sin, from its eternal punishment, and from at least some of its temporal punishment. The sacrament also helps us to grow in God's grace. It strengthens us to avoid sin and to lead holier lives, and reconciles us with the Church which we have wounded by our sins.

Redeemer—Jesus as Savior.

redemption—"buying back"—the rescue or ransom of all of us by Jesus, who laid down His life to set us free from sin; our salvation accomplished by Jesus Christ through His death on the cross.

Regina Coeli—a prayer said during the Easter Season, instead of the Angelus.

relic—part of the body of a saint, an object closely connected with the saint, or something that has been touched to the saint's body (these are honored by the Church).

religious brothers—men who, without becoming priests, dedicate themselves to God in a special way by the religious vows of chastity, obedience and poverty.

religious priests—priests who belong to a religious community and make the vows of poverty, chastity and obedience (not all priest are *religious*; some are called *diocesan*).

religious sisters—women who dedicate themselves to God through the religious vows of chastity, obedience and poverty.

reparation—making up for one's own sins or those of others.

repentance—sorrow for sins and the intention of not sinning again.

resurrection—Jesus' rising from the dead by His own power; the raising of all bodies from the dead at the end of the world, rejoined with their souls by God.

revelation—the truths of religion which God has made known to us through Scripture and Tradition.

reverence—great respect.

right intention—a resolve to act for a good purpose; good will.

right living—applying God's laws with sincerity to our own daily thoughts, words and actions.

rite—the way in which liturgical worship is carried out—that is, the words and actions used.

Rock of Peter—an expression formed from Jesus' words to Peter: "You are Rock, and on this rock I will build my Church" (cf. Matthew 16:18) which means the *Papacy*.

Rosary—a "Gospel prayer" made up of Our Father's, Hail Mary's and Glory's, in which we think about important events in the lives of Jesus and Mary.

S

sacramental—holy things or actions with which the Church asks God to grant us favors, especially spiritual favors.

sacraments—the actions of Jesus—the chief ways in which He gives us His Spirit to make us holy—visible signs of His invisible grace.

Sacred Heart—our Savior, Jesus, especially honored because of His great love, by which He gave His life for us.

sacrifice—giving oneself to God through the sign of offering Him something precious; giving up something or doing something hard out of love.

Sacrifice of Calvary—Jesus' death on the cross for our sins, which is renewed in every Eucharistic Celebration.

saint—a holy person on earth or in heaven, especially someone who grew so close to God on earth that the Church declared him or her a saint after death.

salvation—the condition of being saved (set free from sin and brought to God).

sanctify—to make holy.

sanctifying grace—the grace (gift of God) that is a sharing in His own life and makes us holy, distinguished from such other graces as actual grace (temporary help for our mind and/or will).

save—to set free from sin; to bring to God and heaven.

Savior—Jesus Christ, who died to save everyone who would accept His salvation.

scandal—bad example which leads others to sin.

scapular—two small pieces of cloth, fastened by strings and worn around the neck in front and in back as a sacramental (the most common one being in honor of Mary as Our Lady of Mount Carmel).

sceptre—a staff used by kings as their symbol of authority.

Scripture (or Scriptures)—the written Word of God, the Bible.

seal—a lasting spiritual "mark" or "character."

secularism—the attitude that faith and worship have no place in our lives.

seminarian—someone who is studying to become a priest.

senses (five)—sight, hearing, touch, taste and smell.

separated brethren—our brother Christians (the Eastern Orthodox and Protestants).

Sermon on the Mount—Jesus' preaching of many of the teachings of the New Covenant as recorded in St. Matthew's Gospel, chapters 5 through 7.

sick call—bringing Holy Communion to the ill and infirm (also the sacrament of Reconciliation if a priest is making the sick call).

sin—an offense against God (see mortal sin, venial sin, personal sin, original sin).

slander (calumny)— the sin of harming another person's good name by telling lies or partial truths.

sloth—laziness in work, prayer or other duties.

society—a group of people joined by the same leaders, the same purpose and the same helps for reaching that purpose; all people; all the people of a particular place.

soul—the spirit which together with a body makes up a human being.

spirit—something living but not material.

spiritual works of mercy—to counsel the doubtful, to instruct the ignorant, to admonish the sinner, to comfort the sorrowful, to forgive injuries, to bear wrongs patiently, to pray for the living and the dead.

sponsor—a person who will be responsible for the faith of someone being baptized and/or confirmed.

state of grace—freedom from original and mortal sin; possession of God's grace.

statue—a three-dimensional representation of someone, such as Jesus, Mary, a saint ...which helps us to think of the person while we pray.

sterilization—the process by which a person is made incapable of having children (a sin when done for this purpose).

suicide—the sin of taking one's own life (a mortal sin if the person is in his or her right mind).

Sunday obligation—the responsibility that a Catholic has to attend Mass on Sunday to worship God.

supernatural—above or beyond what is natural. Having to do with God's grace.

superstition—attributing to creatures powers which belong to God alone, by believing in horoscopes, dreams, crystal gazing, charms and the like; by consulting spiritualists; by the use of magic; by satanism, which is invocation of the devil.

T

tabernacle—a boxlike enclosure in which the Blessed Sacrament is kept.

temperance—the cardinal virtue by which a person exercises self-control with regard to food, sex, etc.

temporal punishment—punishment which one is obliged to endure for a time, either in this life or in purgatory, for sins already forgiven.

temptation—something that makes sin attractive.

Ten Commandments—laws given to us by God to help us live in a way worthy of our dignity as human beings and His children.

theological—pertaining to God.

theological virtues—God-given and God-centered habits of doing good—by name, faith, hope and charity.

Tradition—the teachings of Jesus that were not written by the first Christians but passed on from the apostles through their successors. (Tradition was later written down, mainly in the official teachings of the Church.)

transformation—complete change.

Transubstantiation (Mass)—the change that takes place at Mass, when Jesus changes the bread and wine completely into His own Body and Blood.

Trinity—one God in three divine Persons.

Triune God—(see Trinity).

U

universal—for all people, of all places.

universal judgment—the event at the end of the world when God will make known everyones eternal destiny in the presence of all mankind.

universe—sum total of created things.

V

vandal—someone who destroys someone else's property on purpose.

Vatican City—the city (which is also an independent nation) in which the Pope lives.

Vatican Council II—the ecumenical council (world-wide meeting of bishops, called by the Pope) that was held in St. Peter's Basilica, Vatican City, from 1962 to 1965.

veneration—the honor given to Mary and the saints, which is less than the worship, or adoration given to God.

venial sin—a lesser sin or offense against God which weakens our friendship with Him.

Viaticum—Communion given to a person in danger of death; it should be given when the sick person is fully conscious.

Vicar of Christ—the person who takes Jesus' place on earth—the Pope.

victim—whatever is offered to God in sacrifice.

virgin-birth—means that our Lady remained a virgin before, during and after the birth of Christ.

virginity—the moral virtue of an unmarried person who has never sinfully experienced sexual intercourse.

virtues—habits of doing good; habits that are holy (some examples are obedience, patience, charity...).

vocation—God's calling of a person to a particular way of life, especially the priesthood or religious life.

vow—an important promise freely made to God of something very good and pleasing to Him.

W

will—the power to choose.

witness—one who tells or shows what he has seen and/or heard.

witness to Christ—one who learns, lives, loves, stands up for and shares the Faith.

Word of God—the Bible, God's "letter" to us.

works of mercy—good deeds done for others out of love for God and people.

worship—honoring and praising God; offering Him the gift of ourselves in the Mass and in other prayers; believing Him and doing what is right; worship as veneration (not adoration) also given to the angels and saints.

Index

BEHIND
THE SCENES

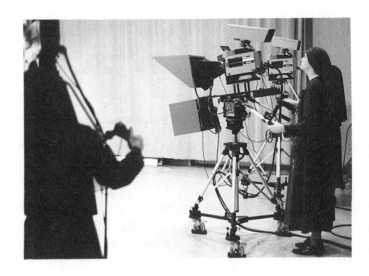

This book was completely written, edited, printed, bound, and produced by the Daughters of St. Paul as part of our communications apostolate.

Our religious Congregation was founded in 1915
to bring
the Word of God
to the people of today.
Catechetics has been
a main thrust of our
apostolic mandate
from the beginning.

Today we have
book and audio-visual centers
in 23 cities and 17 states
of the U.S.,
and in 34 countries
around the world.
And in every location
we are committed
to spreading the message
of Jesus Christ
through the press,
films, audio-visual media,
radio and television,
in fidelity to the Church
and to the charism of our Founder,
the Servant of God,
Father James Alberione (1884-1971).

We are not an ordinary
publishing house,
for our catechetical apostolate
is the fruit of our consecration.
Thus, for us catechetics takes on a
dynamic ecclesial dimension.
And we would like you to know that
you, the religious educator, and
your students are remembered
in the prayers of every
Daughter of St. Paul in our daily
Hour of Adoration before the
Blessed Sacrament.

DAUGHTERS OF ST. PAUL

ALASKA
750 West 5th Ave., Anchorage, AK 99501 **907-272-8183.**
CALIFORNIA
3908 Sepulveda Blvd., Culver City, CA 90230 **213-397-8676.**
1570 Fifth Ave. (at Cedar Street), San Diego, CA 92101 **619-232-1442;**
   619-232-1443.
46 Geary Street, San Francisco, CA 94108 **415-781-5180.**
FLORIDA
145 S.W. 107th Ave., Miami, FL 33174 **305-559-6715; 305-559-6716.**
HAWAII
1143 Bishop Street, Honolulu, HI 96813 **808-521-2731.**
ILLINOIS
172 North Michigan Ave., Chicago, IL 60601 **312-346-4228;**
   312-346-3240.
LOUISIANA
4403 Veterans Memorial Blvd., Metairie, LA 70006 **504-887-7631;**
   504-887-0113.
MASSACHUSETTS
50 St. Paul's Ave., Jamaica Plain, Boston, MA 02130 **617-522-8911.**
Rte. 1, 885 Providence Hwy., Dedham, MA 02026 **617-326-5385.**
MISSOURI
9804 Watson Rd., St. Louis, MO 63126 **314-965-3512; 314-965-3571.**
NEW JERSEY
561 U.S. Route 1, Wick Plaza, Edison, NJ 08817 **908-572-1200;**
   908-572-1201.
NEW YORK
150 East 52nd Street, New York, NY 10022 **212-754-1110.**
78 Fort Place, Staten Island, NY 10301 **718-447-5071; 718-447-5086.**
OHIO
2105 Ontario Street (at Prospect Ave.), Cleveland, OH 44115
   216-621-9427.
PENNSYLVANIA
214 W. DeKalb Pike, King of Prussia, PA 19406 **215-337-1882;**
   215-337-2077.
SOUTH CAROLINA
243 King Street, Charleston, SC 29401 **803-577-0175.**
TEXAS
114 Main Plaza, San Antonio, TX 78205 **512-224-8101.**
VIRGINIA
1025 King Street, Alexandria, VA 22314 **703-549-3806.**
CANADA
3022 Dufferin Street, Toronto, Ontario, Canada M6B 3T5 **416-781-9131.**